Michael Williams

Some London Theatres

Past and present

Michael Williams

Some London Theatres
Past and present

ISBN/EAN: 9783337428945

Printed in Europe, USA, Canada, Australia, Japan

Cover: Foto ©ninafisch / pixelio.de

More available books at **www.hansebooks.com**

SOME LONDON THEATRES

PAST AND PRESENT.

BY

MICHAEL WILLIAMS.

London:

SAMPSON LOW, MARSTON, SEARLE, & RIVINGTON,

CROWN BUILDINGS, 188, FLEET STREET.

1883.

PREFACE.

SOME of the following sketches have already appeared, in another form, elsewhere. The writer does not claim to have been exhaustive in his account of the various theatres set forth, but has rather aimed at reproducing—to the best of his power—the more interesting and important features of their history, whilst, at the same time, connecting these with general facts and *data*. Beyond the period of his own recollection he has endeavoured to verify every incident, great and small, by the most careful and diligent research ; and should the book succeed in winning the approbation of the playgoing public, he hopes, at some future time, to offer another volume for their acceptance.

May, 1883.

CONTENTS.

SOME LONDON THEATRES,

PAST AND PRESENT.

"THE STORY OF OLD SADLER'S WELLS."

AMONGST the many relics of a bygone era, which day by day are becoming gradually effaced, few can show a past of more interest and variety than the old theatre of Sadler's Wells. This edifice, the interior of which was entirely reconstructed in 1879, stands on the site of an orchestra, erected in 1683, by a surveyor of highways, named Sadler, the value of whose property was considerably enhanced, during the same year, through the discovery of a long-forgotten spring of mineral water, by some workmen, when digging for gravel, in the gardens belonging to the house. Malcolm, in his interesting *Londinium Redivivum*, published in 1803, notices an application to the House of Commons, from a former proprietor—probably the younger Forcer—of Sadler's Wells, certifying that this was a place of public entertainment, as early as the reign of Elizabeth. On what grounds

D

the petitioner rested his statement, we have not been able to learn, but it is evident that the spring was known, and resorted to, at a very early period. The monks of Clerkenwell Priory, in particular, were in the habit of frequenting it, and of exacting money, in return for their prayers, from the sick people who came to test its healing powers. At the time of the Reformation, the monks disappeared, and with them the well, which seems to have been covered in, and its identity lost, until accidentally brought to light by the workpeople of Sadler, at an interval of some hundred and forty odd years.

Although never attaining to the fashionable notoriety of the neighbouring Islington Spa—with which Lysons, and Sir John Hawkins, have erroneously confounded it—the new establishment, from being at first respectably conducted, quickly arrived at a certain popularity. To advertise the merits of the re-discovered spring, a small tract was published in 1684, assuming to be "a true and exact account of Sadler's Well; or the New Mineral Waters, lately found at Islington, treating of its nature and virtues, &c., by T. G. (Thomas Guidot), Doctor of Physick." John Evelyn, in his diary, for the 11th of June, 1686, writes : "I went to see Middleton's receptacle of Water, at the New River, and the New Spa Well near." We read also of vocal and instrumental concerts, of posturers, tumblers, and rope-dancers, as supplied for the diversion of the water-drinkers ; of a piper seated upon a shell-work rock, to the strains of whose tabour the visitors might, if it so pleased them, dance ; and of a certain Mrs. Pearson who was engaged to play on the dulcimer,

from five to eight, every summer evening, at the end of
the long walk. Sadler withdrew, towards the end of the
century, in favour of a Mr. Miles, who entered into
partnership with the musician, Francis Forcer. The
place was known, in 1699, as Miles' Musick House, and
upon one occasion in this year was witnessed the dis-
gusting spectacle of a man devouring, for a wager, a live
fowl, "feathers and all." A few years later Sadler's Wells
seems to have resumed its original appellation. Edward
Ward, in his satire, *A Walk to Islington*, written about
this time, describes, with much humour, the amusements
of Sadler's Wells, and tells how the company became
attentive when a vocalist

> "Lady Squab, with her moonified face
> By the side of the organ resumes her old place."

He speaks also of a fiddler in scarlet,

> "Who runs up in *alt*, with a hey-diddle-diddle,
> To show what a fool he can make of a fiddle ;"

followed by a girl of eleven, who performs a sword dance,

> "And further the mob's admiration to kindle,
> She turns on her heel, like a wheel in a spindle ;"

and a youth

> "In dancing a jig lies the chief of whose graces,
> And making strange musick-house monkey-like faces ;"

not forgetting "honest friend Thomas" who officiates in
the twofold capacity of clown, and waiter. These exhibi-

tions were repeated several times during the day, the practice being, when the room was quite full, for some one, purposely stationed at the back, to call out " Is Hiram Fisteman here?" whereupon the entertainment was hastily concluded, and a fresh audience admitted.

Of the visitors the actor Macklin gives an almost contemporaneous account in his reminiscences, and says, " Though we had a mixture of very odd company, there was little or no rioting," significantly adding that " there was a public *then* that kept one another in awe."

To judge by subsequent events, however, this same public, a little later on, must have sadly degenerated. There is extant a very curious tract, dated 1712, and entitled *God's Judgment against Murderers*, being " an account of a cruel and barbarous murther, committed on Thursday night, the 14th of August, at Sadler's Musick-House, near Islington, on the body of Mr. Waite, a lieutenant of a Man-of-War, by one Mr. French, a Lawyer of the Temple." This tract describes Sadler's Wells as " a daily meeting or *rendezvous* of people who go thither to divert themselves; and though 'tis in many very innocent, and in the people of the house, only getting an honest livelihood, yet the method of so doing is apt to draw many unaccountable and disorderly persons to frequent it." Then follows an account of the murder " near the organ-loft." Again we read in the *Weekly Journal*, for 1718, that " Sadler's Wells being lately opened, there is likely to be a great resort of strolling damsels, half-pay officers, peripatetic tradesmen, tars, butchers, and others musically inclined."

Miles died in 1724, and Forcer in 1730. The son of
the latter then carried on the management alone for
thirteen years. Hogarth immortalized the Wells, in 1731,
by introducing a corner of the building, with the old
signboard, into his painting called "Evening." In the
year 1744, the grand jury of Middlesex drew up a
memorial, to the effect that the place " now opened, and
carried on, by John Warren, within this county, is
frequently a resort of great numbers of loose, disorderly
people."

In 1746 Rosoman, whose name still lives in an
adjoining street, became proprietor, and during the next
twenty-six years did much to improve the character of a
place which, for some time past, had certainly been dis-
reputable enough. That its frequenters were now of a
higher grade, we may infer from an advertisement, pro-
mulgated in 1757, to announce that "a horse patrole
will be sent in the New Road this night by Mr. Fielding,
for the protection of the nobility and gentry, who go
from the squares, and that end of the town. The road
to the city will also be properly guarded." Rather earlier,
between 1733-48, the environs were so infested by foot-
pads, that link-boys were in constant attendance, at the
doors of Sadler's Wells, to light people when returning
to their homes, in the more distant streets of Clerkenwell;
and a notice was often appended to the bills, that "there
would be a moonlight." Under Rosoman's direction the
programmes at first consisted, as before, of singing,
dancing, and acrobatic displays; but in 1753 a regular
company was formed, for the representation of burlettas,

musical interludes, and pantomimes. The *Rural Calendar* for June, 1755, says of Sadler's Wells, " this theatre—for such it is— is now so well regulated, under the present manager, that a better company is not anywhere to be met with. The performances by Miss Wilkinson are both justly and universally admired ; and she is attended with great pleasure, even by those who heretofore could not look upon feats of this kind with any degree of patience." Miss Wilkinson appears to have been equally distinguished as an equilibrist, and as a performer on the musical glasses, an entertainment much in vogue at the time. Another celebrity of the period was Maddox, who continued for several seasons to astonish the public by his wonderful and very graceful feats of wire-balancing. In 1763 the famous dancer, and pantomimist, Giuseppe Grimaldi, more familiarly known as Iron-Legs and who had come over to England, from the Netherlands, five · years previously, was engaged as ballet-master. Former Chroniclers of the history of Sadler's Wells have stated that Shakspeare's *Tempest* was given there in 1764. We have heard this questioned. The bills of the day nevertheless testify that *The Tempest,* "an entertainment of music and dancing," was represented. Now, it is a fact that on the 1st of May, in that year, Shakspeare's play, or rather the version of it, in which the text had been altered and diluted, after the fashion then and previously prevalent, by Dryden, was actually given at Drury Lane, for the benefit of Signor Grimaldi, and the probability is that this edition was subsequently transferred to the boards of the summer theatre. In the annals of a house which long afterwards—under the auspices of Phelps and Greenwood—won such well-deserved fame for its revivals of the Shakspearian drama, the circumstance, and its bearings, should not be passed over without comment.

" Jemmy " Warner divided with the elder Grimaldi, the post of leading clown, at this time, and for several years onwards. Rosoman replaced the original wooden theatre, in 1765, by a new one of brick; and this, although altered and enlarged at various times, later on, remained virtually the same up to within a year or two of the present date. This manager was also the founder of a convivial society, entitled the "Sadler's Wells Club," which held its meetings at the Sir Hugh Mydelton tavern, opposite the theatre. There might long be seen, in the bar of this tavern, a picture of the club, in which Rosoman was depicted, surrounded by members of his company, and other friends, amongst whom the most conspicuous —according to tradition—were Maddox, the wire-dancer, Greenwood, father of the scene-painter, and Davenport, master of the elder Mathews. On recent inquiry—in the autumn of 1878—we found that the picture had been sold, some time ago, and the one which replaces it is probably a copy of Hogarth's " Midnight Modern Conversation."

After the retirement of Rosoman—who died, it is said, worth forty thousand pounds—in 1772, the property was held, for many subsequent years, in shares, and among the tenants were Tom King—the comedian, and original Sir Peter Teazle, Dr. Cantwell, and Lord Ogleby—

Wroughton, Hughes, Coates, Siddons [1]—husband of Mrs
Siddons—Charles Dibdin, the elder, and his two sons,
Andrews, Barfoot, and Arnold.   The active management
was entrusted to King from 1772 to 1782, and afterwards
successively to Wroughton, Hughes, Lonsdale, and
Charles Dibdin the younger.   In 1776 a dance, the
egg-dance, which dated from the reign of Queen Elizabeth,
was introduced by a Master Lascelles Williamson, who
was a pupil of the elder Grimaldi, and afterwards married his daughter.   The celebrated Harlequin, James
Byrne, father of the subsequently well-known chore-
graphist, Oscar Byrne, was ballet-master during this and
the previous year.   The year 1781 will be ever memorable in the annals of Sadler's Wells for the first appearance
—on Easter Monday, April 16th—of one who is said to
have been the greatest clown that ever lived—Joseph
Grimaldi.   According to the parochial registers of St.
Clement Danes, Grimaldi, son of the aforesaid " Iron-
Legs," was born on the 18th of December, 1778.   With
the exception of one summer, that of 1817—his winters

---

[1] The money was, of course, supplied by the latter.   Of
Mrs. Siddons's investment in proprietary shares at Sadler's
Wells, Madame D'Arblay, equally well known as Miss
Burney, the authoress of *Evelina*, writes in her Diary for
1797, " I could not hear of it without some amusement.   It
seemed so extraordinary a combination—so degrading a one
indeed—that of the first tragic actress, the living Melpomene,
and something so burlesque as Sadler's Wells."   From which
we may infer that the place was held in no exalted estimation
by the society, literary or aristocratic, of that particular
period.

were occupied at Drury Lane and Covent Garden—he was attached to the theatre for a period of forty-seven years. Rising from small beginnings, he finally, by his industry, perseverance, and attention to his professional duties, reached a supremacy, in his own peculiar line, which old playgoers assert to have never since been equalled, or even approached. The other most prominent members of the company, from 1780 to 1800, were the comedians, Mrs. Harlowe, Dighton, and "Jew" Davies; the pantomimists, Bologna (father and two sons), Placido, Paul Redigé, surnamed the Little Devil, with his wife, La Belle Espagnole, Richer, Madame St. Amande, and Dubois. The insecurity of the approaches to Sadler's Wells towards the end of the last century may be inferred from a play-bill of June, 1783, wherein it is stated that "patrols of horse and foot are stationed from Sadler's Wells Gate, along the New Road, to Moorfields; also to St. John's Street, and across the Spa fields, to Rosoman Row, from the hours of eight to eleven."

In 1784 a troupe of performing dogs proved so great an attraction, as to realize, for the managers, a profit of ten thousand pounds. Miss Romanzini, afterwards better known as the favourite ballad-singer, Mrs. Bland, appeared in 1786, and Braham—then a boy, Master Abrahams—in 1788. Possibly the best engraving extant of Sadler's Wells, is the one published in 1792, by the scene-painter, Andrews. Save for the word "gallery," observable over a side door, and a sign-board high up on one of the gables, the building, standing by the New River, and overshadowed by trees, has here more the look of some quaint old suburban manor-house, than of an ordinary London theatre. The Duke and Duchess of York visited it this season, and the attendance, generally, was of a superior description. Richer revived the egg-dance in 1793, and in 1794 the ballet-pantomime of *Valentine and Orson*, in which Dubois, and Grimaldi, were successively so famous, was first produced. Of Dubois, Malcolm tells us that " Mr. Dubois, a veteran on the stage of nearly forty years, bears away the palm from all without exception, to whom speech is denied. His talents are of the most versatile description, acting on the same evening a complete fool, and a character of dignity, with equal truth. He is particularly happy in portraying a dark, malicious, and ambitious part. The transitions in his countenance from smiles to threats, from approbation to abhorrence, are masterly performances. I have seen him—when pursued by a person whom he had injured, and whose parent he had murdered, disguised as a ghost—betray such dreadful emotions of terror, horror, guilt, confusion, and revenge, that I could almost suppose the fiction approached reality. His performance of Orson, in the ballet before mentioned, displayed a thorough insight into human nature, debased. He mixed the tricks and sagacity of the monkey, with the gleams of matured reason, so judiciously, that an enlightened audience would have been delighted. So in a recent character of a Moor, he is to fight, in single combat—after the defeat of his adherents—with their conqueror. His motions are no longer European ; they are those of the savage ; grimaces, glaring search for the most vulnerable part of his antagonist's body, and endeavours to fix a firm footing, to dart, like a tiger, on his prey, characterize every muscle." Dubois was evidently as unequalled, in his own day, as Grimaldi subsequently became ; and it is clear that the latter who, in early life, was constantly associated on the boards with this celebrated *mime*, must have formed his style on the same lines, since the first Grimaldi died, in 1788, whilst the son was still far too young to have derived much benefit from his father's tuition.

Another remarkable event in the chronicles of the theatre occurred in 1801, namely, the first appearance in a speaking part—he had already played Cupid in a ballet at the King's Theatre, in the Haymarket—of a juvenile wonder, Master Carey, who recited the principal speech of Rolla, in Sheridan's *Pizarro*. This boy was the great-grandson of Henry Carey — natural son of George Savile Carey, Marquis of Halifax—who at an earlier date had written and composed many musical pieces for the theatre. The more important of these are now forgotten, but the little song of " Sally in our Alley," so touching in its homely pathos, will continue to live as long as English ballad-singing lasts. Some years later, this young Carey developed into the great tragedian—Edmund Kean.

Pony races were tried in 1802, and the African traveller, Belzoni, exhibited some feats of herculean strength as a gymnast, " The Patagonian Samson," in the following year. The principal of these feats was to walk round the stage, supporting on his shoulder a pyramidal frame-work, on which rested eleven men, the topmost of whom reached to the flies. Upon one occasion the stage gave way, owing to their weight, and precipitated the giant with his incumbrances into the water beneath. From 1804, for many years onwards, Sadler's Wells became noted for its aquatic pieces, in the progress of which the entire flooring, was drawn up to the roof, to make way for a huge tank, filled by means of pipes connected with the New River. In this tank, naval fights and other maritime sensations were enacted, and *The Battle of the Nile*, *The Siege of Gibraltar*, *Philip and his Dog*, with other productions of a similar kind, gained an extraordinary popularity, as was recorded by Greenwood in his Rhyming Reminiscences :—

"Attraction was needed the town to engage,
So Dick emptied the river that year on the stage ;
The house overflow'd, and became quite the ton,
And the Wells for some seasons went swimmingly on."

The Dick referred to was the manager, Hughes, and father-in-law of Grimaldi. Before he ascended the throne, William the Fourth, probably in compliment to these aquatic pieces, was a great patron of Sadler's Wells. The words, "Under the patronage of His Royal Highness, the Duke of Clarence," were at this time and for many years afterwards, frequently at the head of the play-bills. The night of Thursday, the 15th of October, 1807, witnessed a fearful catastrophe, arising from the panic caused by a false alarm of fire. In the rush to the doors, twenty-three people were suffocated, and many more severely injured. The name of Hartland, a fine pantominist, appeared in 1810, as also that of Cobham, a very striking actor, and an unsuccessful rival of Kean. Barnes and Ellar were also in the company at this time.

On the occasion of Grimaldi's benefit, in October, 1814, his son made his *début*, playing Friday to the Robinson Crusoe of his father. Joseph-Samuel-William Grimaldi, professionally known as "Mr. J. S. Grimaldi," Grimaldi's son, by his second wife, Mary Bristow, was born on the 21st of November, 1802. For several years after the date of his first appearance he was—partly, perhaps, owing to the *prestige* of his father's name—rarely without an engagement at one or other of the leading metropolitan houses. He is said to have inherited much of the family talent, but was too unsteady, in private life, to improve it by study, or to ultimately maintain his position. He was dismissed from one theatre after another, and died, from the effects of a drunken brawl, on the 11th of December, 1832. In 1816 Grimaldi first played his finest, but also his most difficult and fatiguing part, Orson, in *Valentine and Orson*. Paulo, son of "La Belle Espagnole," and the "Little Devil," was engaged to replace Grimaldi as clown, in 1817, but the latter returned in the following year, and from this time was a shareholder in the theatre. George Wieland, also another highly-gifted pantomimist, made his first appearance on the stage, at the age of five years, at Sadler's Wells, in 1817. Grimaldi introduced his famous song, "Hot Codlings"—in the pantomime of *The Talking Bird*—for the first time, in 1819. Howard Payne, author of the tragedy of *Brutus*, was lessee in 1820, and Egerton, of Covent Garden, during the three following years, when the stately Mrs. Egerton played the leading parts. Wilkinson, Keeley, Vale, Wallbourne, and Miss Scott, were also in the company. The ill-fated queen, Caroline of Brunswick, wife of George the Fourth, visited the place in 1821, when the performances consisted of *The Mountain Hut*, the burletta *Jacintha*, and the pantomime of *Harlequin at Home*. In 1824 Miss Vincent, later on so celebrated for her impersonations of domestic and melodramatic heroines, at the various minor theatres, but at this date a strikingly beautiful child of ten years old, appeared, with marked success in an occasional piece, *The Actress of All Work*. In 1825 the veteran, Thomas Dibdin, the author of so many of the Sadler's Wells pieces, assumed the active management, his wife playing the leading parts. Mrs. Fitzwilliam also had an engagement, and for the first time the house was opened for the winter season. The aeronaut, Mrs. Graham, ascended in a balloon from the grounds, on the 21st of June, 1826, and during this and the ensuing summer ponyracing constituted the chief attraction. A very good low comedian, Mr. W. H. Williams, was also acting here.

On Monday, the 28th of March, 1828, Grimaldi, who had long been incapacitated, through illness, from regularly following his profession, took his farewell of the Islington public, as Hock, in the romance of *The Sixes*, and this, with the exception of another benefit, on a larger scale, got up by his friends, at Covent Garden,

in July of the same year, was his last appearance on the
stage. From this date, although occasionally assisting
in the stage-management of the theatre—only three
weeks before his death, he superintended the reproduction of the famous pantomime, *Mother Goose*—he lived
in retirement, and expired, at 33, Southampton Street,
Pentonville, on the 31st of May, 1837. He was interred
by the side of his old friend and work-fellow, Charles
Dibdin, in the burial-ground of the neighbouring St.
James's Church, and his grave-stone bears the following
inscription : —

```
          SACRED
      TO THE MEMORY OF
  MR. JOSEPH GRIMALDI,
      Who departed this life
          May 31, 1837.
      Aged fifty-eight years.
```

At the foot of the grave is another stone inscribed
" Grimaldi, 1837." With " Joe" Grimaldi apparently
the old order of clowns became extinct. Certainly none,
since his day, have attained to anything like the same
eminence or distinction. For Grimaldi, as we have
been assured by his old contemporary and intimate
friend, the once famed theatrical engraver, Henry Brown
—still living in the present year, 1881—was no mere
clown, he was a great comedian born, and in this lay
the secret of his superiority over all his rivals in this
branch of the profession. And a really kind heart, an

even temper, combined with a most child-like simplicity of character, caused him to be as universally beloved in private as he was admired in public; whilst the statement, found after death amongst his papers, that in the solitary hours of declining life, he could not recollect one single instance in which he had intentionally wronged man, woman, or child, may have well found a ready echo in the breast of every one who ever knew him.

On Boxing-night, 1828, Tom Matthews, the favourite pupil of Grimaldi, and the inheritor of many of his traditions, came out as clown in a new pantomime, *The Hag of the Forest Raven.* In August, 1829, a version of Douglas Jerrold's popular Surrey drama, *Black-Eyed Susan,* was produced, in which William was played by Campbell, and Susan by Mrs Wilkinson. In 1830 the attention of the public was directed to the dancing of Mrs. Searle and her pupils. One of these, a young girl named Laura Bell, a few years later grew into one of the loveliest women that ever graced the English stage —Mrs. Honey. A very fine melodramatic actor, Mr. Freer, also appeared as Sir Giles Overreach. Mr. W. H. Williams and Mrs. Fitzwilliam were the joint lessees in 1832, and a vaudeville, *The Pet of the Petticoats,*[1] had a considerable run.

The names of Almar, Osbaldiston, Nelson Lee, and Robert Honner were subsequently associated, in turn, with the direction, but did little or nothing to enhance its reputation. On the contrary, the theatre gradually

[1] The music by John Barnett, composer of *The Mountain Sylph.*

sank to so low an ebb, that any attempt to improve its
fortunes was at last looked upon as hopeless. True that
Mrs. Waylett sang in 1836, that Junius Brutus Booth
"starred" in 1837. Mrs. Glover, too, played the Nurse
to the Juliet of Mrs. W. West, and the Romeo of George
Bennett, on one night in this year. T. P. Cooke appeared as William, in *Black-Eyed Susan*, on Tuesday, the
18th of December, 1838, for the benefit of Mr. Honner.
Elton also played in 1840; and Ducrow brought his
horses out here in 1842. As years rolled by, however,
it seemed more and more evident that with the retirement of Grimaldi, the old glory had departed. never to
return. But happier days were yet in store, when in the
spring of 1844, the great actor, Phelps, assumed the
management; and we can affirm, without any hesitation,
that the next eighteen years, during which he presided
over its destinies, form, in truth, the best and brightest
page in the history of old Sadler's Wells. For the
greater part of this time Mr. Phelps was connected in
partnership * with Mr. Greenwood, a former lessee—for a

* Mr. Greenwood's name first appears in connexion with
Sadler's Wells in May, 1841, at which date he filled the post
of acting-manager to the then lessee, Mr. Robert Honner.
The lesseeship would seem to have been transferred to him
about the month of August, 1842, and he thenceforward conducted it, on purely minor theatre principles, with the assistance of the late Mr. Henry Marston, in the double capacity
of leading actor and stage-manager, until Whitsuntide, 1844.
On the alteration in the management at that period, Mr.
Phelps was appointed stage-manager, Mr. Warner treasurer,
and Mr. Greenwood resumed his old position of acting-

C

short term—of the house; and henceforth, whilst the
refined taste and histrionic talents of the former raised
the artistic credit of the enterprise to the highest point,
the sound judgment and business capacity of the latter
served to maintain its financial prosperity. Their task
was, at first, no easy one. Melodrama of the coarsest
type had long been the fare offered to a class of frequenters, in themselves so utterly vicious, that no respectable tradesman would dream of taking his wife or
daughters to the place. The lessees had not only to
purify the nature of the performances, they had also to
unmake, as well as to create, their audience. With what
indomitable courage and resolution they set about their
reforms, on both sides of the curtain, is well known;
and so thoroughly did they carry them out that in time
this obscure little temple of the Drama could boast not
only of the most intelligent, but—beyond comparison—
the most intellectual pit of any theatre in London. It
was no uncommon circumstance, during the run of some
special revival, to see the entire pit and boxes diligently
following the text from printed copies of the play. Nor
was Sadler's Wells any longer dependent on merely *local*
patronage for its support. The "nobility and gentry

manager. So little hope was entertained by the new lessees
in the permanent attraction of the legitimate drama, that a
new melodrama, of the blue-fire species, had been prepared,
and was actually underlined in the opening playbill to take
the place of *Macbeth*, in case the tragedy of Shakspeare
should fail, after a fair trial, to command remunerative
audiences. This fact was communicated to the writer by
Mr. Greenwood a few months before his decease.

from the squares," of Rosoman's old-fashioned advertisement, now found their analogy in the more modern
inhabitants of Mayfair and Belgravia, who came out in
numbers to a spot, of which, possibly, many of them had
hitherto scarcely even heard, whilst all that was most
distinguished in the literary world, made a point of being
present on every " first night " at " the Wells." And
no higher compliment could well have been paid to any
management than the one addressed to it by Macready,
when, in a letter written to the late Lord Chief Justice
Pollock, in 1856, he remarked, " I believe we must look
for the drama, if we really wish to find it, in that remote
suburb of Islington."

We have been informed that the lessees originally intended to bring out the entire series of Shakspeare's plays,
and it is a fact that they did succeed in producing thirty-
one of them. These were *Macbeth*—with the inter-
polated scenes from Middleton's old play, *The Witch*,
and Locke's music, on the opening night, Whit-Monday,
the 27th of May, 1844 ; but afterwards strictly in accordance with the original text—*Othello, The Merchant of
Venice, King John, Hamlet, King Richard III.*—with the
original text, in lieu of Colley Cibber's version, which was,
however, represented at one period—*King Henry VIII,
King Lear, A Winter's Tale, The First Part of King
Henry IV., Julius Cæsar, Romeo and Juliet, Measure for
Measure, The Tempest, Cymbeline, As You Like It, Twelfth
Night, The Merry Wives of Windsor, Coriolanus, Much
Ado about Nothing, Antony and Cleopatra, Timon of
Athens, All's Well that Ends Well, The Second Part of*

King Henry IV., *King Henry V.*, *A Midsummer Night's Dream*, *Pericles, Prince of Tyre*, *Taming of the Shrew*— with Phelps as Christopher Sly—*Two Gentlemen of Verona*, *Comedy of Errors*, and *Love's Labour Lost*. We have been told by Mr. Greenwood that it was also, at one time, in contemplation to bring out *Troilus and Cressida*, but that the idea was abandoned, owing to the difficulty of finding a sufficient number of actors suitable for the various Grecian heroes. The following works, by other old dramatists, contemporaneous with Shakspeare, were also presented : *The Honest Man's Fortune*, *A King and No King*, and *Rule a Wife and have a Wife*, of Beaumont and Fletcher ; the same authors' *Maid's Tragedy*, modernized by Sheridan Knowles under the title of *The Bridal ; The City Madam, The Fatal Dowry*, and *A New Way to Pay Old Debts*, of Massinger ; *A Woman Never Vex't*, of Rowley ; *Venice Preserved*, of Otway ; and *The Duchess of Malfi*, of old John Webster. To these might be added a long list of plays by Lytton, Byron, Knowles, Talfourd, Kotzebue, Pococke, Rowe, Leigh Hunt, Sheridan, Cumberland, Colman, Cibber, Howard Payne, Vanbrugh, Inchbald, Goldsmith, Holcroft, Bickerstaffe, Tobin, Centlivre, Maturin, Milman, Fielding, Macklin, and others, amongst which Cumberland's *Wheel of Fortune*, Macklin's *Man of the World*, *The Miser* of Fielding, *The Fop's Fortune* of Colley Cibber, *The Provoked Husband* of Sir John Vanbrugh, *Arden of Feversham*, by Rowe, and *The Good-natured Man*, by Oliver Goldsmith, might all be cited as theatrical curiosities, owing to the rarity of their revival, elsewhere.

Another, *The Castle Spectre*, of "Monk" Lewis, given several times in 1849, had, in its time, an immense popularity, and from the romantic interest of the plot, to say nothing of the opportunities for ghostly effects, which it presents, is quite worth the attention of our theatrical managers, to-day. Many new dramas were also written expressly for the house; and of these, *Hamilton of Both-wellhaugh*, by Selous, *Garcia, or the Noble Error*, by F. G. Tomline; *Feudal Times*, *The Gowrie Plot*, and *John Saville of Haystead*, by the Reverend James White; and lastly *The Fool's Revenge*, by Tom Taylor, were all far above the average of new plays. The only translation from the modern French was a version of Casimir Delavigne's *Louis XI.*, given, at the earnest request of his patrons, by Mr. Phelps, in 1861. The same year saw another departure from the legitimate, in the shape of a two-act piece—*Doing for the Best*, by Rophino Lacy—in which, as the humble artisan of domestic drama, the actor showed that he could mesmerize his audience, to the full as much, as he had ever done, in the finest works of our standard authors.

For the representation of the above repertory, a company was gradually formed, as a body, it would seem, at no period of transcendent excellence, but which had the merit—and that, in no ordinary degree—of working, on all occasions, thoroughly well together. Until Mr. and Mrs. Bancroft metamorphosed the old Queen's Theatre in Tottenham Street, the French word *ensemble*—for which our language offers no equivalent—was never more happily realized, on the English stage, than during the days of the Phelps and Greenwood dynasty, at Sadler's Wells. It was not that a collection of stars was to be met with, but that all, high and low, engaged, were carefully taught, at rehearsal, to abstain, as far as possible, from individual prominence, and to aim rather at carrying out each his separate work, so as to blend it with the rest, in one harmonious whole. The conception of the author, not the exhibition of this or that performer, was always the first thing to be regarded here. No one was ever engaged in whom the lessees failed to detect at least the germ of a Shaksperian talent, and this, when once found, was forthwith developed with untiring assiduity. To have played with Phelps, at Sadler's Wells, is yet the proudest boast of those who survive from his old company; and many of our best actors and actresses have owed their fame to the training which they received, in early life, at "The Theatre," as it is still affectionately termed by the Islingtonians. In the *Illustrated London News*, for Saturday, the 9th of January, 1847, there is an engraving of the green-room at Sadler's Wells, with Mr. Phelps, and a portion of his company, as constituted at the time—with the names underlined—dressed for their parts in *The Merchant of Venice.* Whether the older picture of Rosoman may have suggested it, we cannot tell, but, for playgoers, the print has already become invested with an interest scarcely less powerful than the other.

In a management extending over eighteen years, many changes necessarily occurred, but it would be unfair, in this summary of its doings, to refrain from enumerating the names of some, at least, of those who successively assisted in supporting its reputation. Among the best remembered were Mrs. Warner, for the first two years associated in the direction with the other proprietors, and herself one of the finest tragic actresses of her day ; Mrs. Henry Marston, since Mrs. Glover's retirement the best duenna on the stage ; Mrs. Brougham, Mrs. Barrett, Mrs. Ternan, Mrs. Herman Vezin—at first better known as Mrs. Charles Young—and the Misses Glyn, Fitzpatrick, Laura Addison, Cooper, Goddard, Atkinson, Fanny Vining, Baddeley, Margaret Eburne, Julia St. George, Sarah Lyons, Jenny Marston, Edith Heraud, Hughes —now Mrs. Gaston Murray—Wyatt, Heath, Murray, Lebatt, and Fanny Huddart ; together with Messrs. Creswick, Henry Marston, George Bennett, Thomas Hailes Lacy, Hudson, Younge, Hoskyns, Barrett, Williams, Fenton, George Scharfe, J. W. Ray, Lewis Ball, Frederick Robinson, Belford, Mortimer, Morelli, Villiers, Branson, Henry Mellon, Lunt, Waller, Henry Nye, T. C. Harris, Butler, Graham, Edmund Phelps, and Herman Vezin.

In all pertaining to the *mise-en-scène*, nothing could exceed the care and accuracy bestowed on every production, and more especially on the successive Shaksperian revivals. Stage-decoration was employed to enhance, but never to impede, the action ; to adorn, but never to obscure, the plot. Splendour was never wanting where splendour was due ; but it was a splendour invariably tempered by the purest taste. For, as was justly pointed out by an eminent critic—Henry Morley of the *Examiner* —of the day, Shakspeare's plays were always *poems*, as performed at Sadler's Wells. And as examples of the poetic spirit in which they were approached, none better could be adduced than the exquisite *Midsummer Night's Dream*, revived in 1853, *The Tempest* in 1847, and, with still finer effect, in 1855. *Timon of Athens*, revived in 1851, and again in 1856, forms another case in point. On the other hand, *Pericles, Prince of Tyre*, brought out in 1854, and which, from its very nature, came to be treated—however artistically—chiefly as a *spectacle*, was also, strange to say, the only one that failed to realize a pecuniary success.

The partnership of Messrs. Greenwood and Phelps expired early in 1860, and after carrying on the theatre for the next two years single-handed, the latter finally retired from the management on the 15th of March, 1862, when *The City Madam* of Massinger was performed. In the following November Mr. Phelps returned for a short engagement, and, on the night of his benefit. delivered an address, in which, after expressing a hope that he had fulfilled the promise made on starting, of raising the taste of his audiences by the exalted character of the entertainments, he added, "The amusements of the people are a very important item in the composition of our social system. Dramatic representations have stood, and, I believe, always *will* stand, in the foremost rank of those amusements. It is surely better, then, that the young who are so easily led, and so strongly impressed, by them, should receive their impressions from the plays of Shakspeare, rather than from sensation dramas and translations from the French, of questionable morality."

The audience, which Mr. Phelps addressed, was a strictly
representative one, since it comprised many of the inhabitants of the neighbourhood who had grown up during
his management, and had formed their taste for the
drama, within the walls of his theatre. It is unnecessary,
therefore, to add how heartily they indorsed such senti-
ments, and how warmly they cheered their old favourite
on the conclusion of his speech.

From this date the star of Sadler's Wells steadily
waned. A Miss Lucette attempted to reintroduce a style
of performance, such as burletta and other light musical
pieces, similar to those which had been found attractive
about a hundred years before, and, as might have been
anticipated, failed utterly. Then Mr. Edgar became the
lessee, and with the help of his wife—Miss Marriott, a
very good actress—preserved to some extent the traditions
of his great precursors—without their *school.* The house
completed the first centenary of its existence in 1865, and
in August of the following year, a temporary tenant,
Mr. J. Arnold Cave, celebrated the event—although a
year after time—by a revival of the once popular pantomime of *Mother Goose,* in the old days so closely associated, here and at Covent Garden, with the name and
fame of Grimaldi. Mr. Cave himself played the title *rôle*
in Dibdin's introduction, given in its integrity. The
characters in the harlequinade, which had been partly
remodelled, consisted of Mr. Lawrence (clown), Mr.
Skinner (pantaloon), Mr. Paulo (harlequin), and Miss
Brandon (columbine). The *skeleton* scene—much older
than the pantomime itself, and invented, it is said, by the

father of Grimaldi—was retained, and the whole was produced under the superintendence of the veteran Tom Matthews. Mr. Edgar died in 1871, and those—unnecessary to particularize by name—who succeeded him, only served, by their method of carrying it on, to bring the place more and more into contempt. Sadler's Wells was converted into a skating-rink. It was repaired, and talked of for a music-hall. It was pronounced insecure, and shut up altogether. Finally, in January, 1878, the lowest depth of degradation was apparently reached, when its classic precincts became—*actually*—the scene of a *prize-fight !*

At length, when every hope of its resuscitation appeared to have fled, Mrs. Bateman, who, in conjunction with her lamented husband, had for some years been conducting the Lyceum on much the same principles as those which marked the reign of Greenwood and Phelps, having recently parted with her lease of that theatre to Mr. Henry Irving, came forward as the purchaser. It being simply impossible to open the house in its existing condition of ruin and decay, Mrs. Bateman decided to rebuild it entirely, as far as the interior was concerned; and by an odd coincidence, the week in which the workmen commenced their alterations was the one also which closed the life of her most gifted predecessor. On Wednesday, the 6th of November, 1878, Samuel Phelps —born at Devonport on the 13th of February, 1804— breathed his last, at a house called Coopershall, near Epping. It would be unfitting, then, to conclude our sketch of this famous old playhouse without paying some brief tribute to the memory of one whose name was so long identified with many of its most cherished triumphs. We may in truth assert that Mr. Phelps was not only the finest tragedian—he was the soundest, the most learned, and the most conscientious actor that the present generation has ever known. That he was equally great in every part can no more be said of Phelps, han of any other member of the profession, which he so long, and so strikingly, adorned. He had, in fact, his strong and weak points, his strokes of genius, his crudities and mannerisms. In every character, however, which this truly great artist attempted, his reading invariably bore the stamp of most careful study, united to a scrupulous regard for the author's meaning, and a strict adherence to the author's text. To these was added, in rare perfection, that fine and stately method of elocution which, we are told, was the leading characteristic of the old school, and which is now so little cultivated as to be almost extinct. We are unable to speak from our own experience, of that period—the eighteen years of public service at Sadler's Wells Theatre—during which the powers of Phelps must have been in their prime. But in later life, and at the West End houses, when something of physical strength may have been opined, rather than felt, to have departed, we can recall his Shylock, Henry the Fourth, and Justice Shallow, his Falstaff, Malvolio, and Bottom, in addition to Job Thornberry, Mr. Oakley, James the Sixth—in Halliday's *King of Scots*—Dr. Cantwell, Lord Ogleby, and best of all, perhaps, his inimitable Sir Pertinax Macsycophant, as so many delineations of truth, and high art, in acting, the like of which, on our own stage at least, we may never hope to see again.

On the Wednesday following his death, the remains of Phelps were interred in the cemetery at Highgate, and were attended to the grave by a large concourse of his professional brethren, amongst whom, at this lapse of time, might still be recognized many of his old company. The most prominent of these were Mr. Henry Marston, Mr. George Bennett, Mr. Fenton, Mr. Villiers, Mr. Morelli, Mr. Herman Vezin, and his old partner, Mr. Greenwood. The position which the last-named—an intellectual and highly-cultivated man—filled in the memorable enterprise before recorded, has always appeared to us greatly underrated. Mr. Greenwood was as well read in, and as intimately acquainted with, all the beauties of the old dramatists, as Mr. Phelps, and, though himself no actor, he was unerring in his estimate of the acting of others. The selection of the plays, and of the company to perform in them, lay as much with one manager as with the other, whilst the invention and getting-up of the Christmas pantomime—a time-honoured institution which even Shakspeare failed to oust—was exclusively the duty of the former. Furthermore, the all-important department of the treasury, and that most essential balancing of receipts and expenditure, without which any management, no matter how elevated, would very soon go to the wall, was entrusted entirely to Mr. Greenwood, whose duties will thus be seen to have been to the full as onerous as those of his more renowned coadjutor. The actual training of the performers, on the other hand, of necessity devolved upon Phelps, and the consequent realization of that all-round excellence which invariably distinguished every production, was due to his unwearied patience and industry alone. Each, therefore, will be understood to have borne his full share in the good work which Mrs. Bateman, assisted by her daughters, is about, at an interval of seventeen years, to resume. The venture is indeed a bold, and, in some respects, a hazardous one ; but, if we may judge by the genuinely artistic spirit which pervaded the whole course of her directorate at the Lyceum, this lady will readily command the sympathies of all who value the dignity, and respectability, of the stage. It seems certain, from foregone experience, that Mrs. Bateman will only endeavour to deserve success by purely legitimate means. We trust that she may meet with the fullest extent of such success, and that by the results effected in the New, she may revive—she will never surpass—the glories of Old Sadler's Wells.

To the above, written in February, 1879, the following additional notes may be of interest. Mr. Greenwood followed his late partner to his rest, early in the ensuing spring, and on Thursday, October 9, in the same year, Mrs. Bateman, having, surmounted the preliminary dif- culties of building and fitting-up, opened New Sadler's Wells—new only so far as the interior was concerned —with Pocock's old musical drama, *Rob Roy*, produced with much care and completeness, and with Mr. Walter

Bentley, a very rising young actor, in the title *rôle*.　In
addition to enacting Meg Merrilies, Miss Bateman (Mrs.
Crowe) delivered an introductory address, voluntarily
contributed by Tom Taylor, the various points of which,
notably the allusions to Grimaldi, Greenwood, and
" brave old Phelps," were warmly responded to by an
audience which filled the handsome new theatre to overflowing.　New Sadler's Wells, thus auspiciously started,
was conducted with much spirit by Mrs. Bateman until
her death, which occurred, after a very brief illness,[4] early
in the present year, and whilst the arduous task, which
she had so bravely undertaken, of re-establishing its fortunes was still only half accomplished.　In her brief
tenure, however—and exclusive of the summer months,
when the house was under-let to travelling companies—
she had already gone far to revive the ancient *prestige*,
producing, successively, Shakspeare's *Macbeth*, *Othello*,
Romeo and Juliet, Sheridan's *School for Scandal*, Holcroft's
Road to Ruin, Sheridan Knowles's *William Tell* and *The
Hunchback*, Lord Lytton's *Lady of Lyons*, Tom Taylor's
historical play, *Clancarty*, and Mrs. Lovell's delightful
Ingomar.　These plays were supported by her three
daughters, Miss Bateman (Mrs. Crowe), Miss Isabel
Bateman, and Miss Virginia Francis—all admirable in
their respective lines—Miss Carlisle, Miss Maud Irvine,
Mrs. W. Sydney, and Mrs. Charles Calvert ; Messrs. Her-
man Vezin, Charles Warner, Charles Kelly, W. H. Vernon,
Walter Bentley, Talbot, Pennington, E. H. Brooke, Ed-

[4] On Thursday, 13th of January, 1881.

mund Lyons, Robert Lyons, W. F. Windham, John Archer, Fosbrooke, Clifford Harrison, E. Cotte, Walter Brooks, A. Redwood, Wheatcroft, Rowland Buckstone, and William Farren, jun. She had also brought out—on Boxing Night, 1879—a pantomime, *The Forty Thieves*, with a really good clown, of the old-fashioned sort, Mr. Benham—styled in the bills, "The modern Grimaldi"—and, in the following April, an American drama of strong interest, *The Danites*, by Bronson Howard; the plot of which was founded on an incident of Mormon life, and the scene laid in California. The pantomime, though amusing and clever—too clever, perhaps, since much of its wit seemed over the heads of the audience—was a failure. *The Danites*, beautifully mounted, and capitally acted by Mr. McKeen Ranken, with his American company, proved a decided hit, and not only brought money to the treasury, but became a town-talk. On professional grounds, alone, Mrs. Bateman's loss is to be deplored, since she had already done quite enough at Sadler's Wells to show what, under the fostering influence of public support, she might hereafter have been expected to achieve. In private life, as an excellent mother and a very good woman, she will long be sincerely mourned by all who knew her. The theatre, having remained closed for a few nights after her decease, was reopened by Miss Isabel Bateman, with the co-operation of her sisters, and in their hands, we are informed, it will permanently remain. They have the sympathy and good wishes of the public with them, for it is certain that as long as Sadler's Wells continues under their direction, so long will it be made an influence for good in the neighbourhood, and its management be characterized by judgment, intelligence, and good taste.

————

Miss Isabel Bateman continued to carry on the house, during the summer months, and then gave up the management. Mr. F. B. Chatterton—a former lessee of Drury Lane—opened it in October, 1881, with a new melodrama, *The Foundlings*, founded by Mr. Leopold Lewis, on the old French piece, *Les Dames de la Halle.* Mr. Chatterton's venture, however, did not answer, and he relinquished it, rather suddenly, early in 1882. After remaining closed, for a few weeks, a new tenant was obtained, in Mr. Matt Robson, in whose hands the theatre has since remained. Mr. Robson's system appeals almost entirely to local patronage, but under his direction New Sadler's Wells has been conducted with perfect respectability, and is now, we understand, a very thriving and prosperous speculation.

SOMETHING ABOUT OLD HIGHBURY BARN.

HIGHBURY BARN was originally the home-farm—the word *barn* signifying farm, or dairy-house—attached to the ancient manor-house of Highbury or Newington Barrow.

The manor-house of Highbury stood upon the site of a summer camp, formed by the Romans in the vicinity of one of their great military roads—Herman Street—leading to London, and hence its second denomination of Neweton, or Newington, Barrow may probably have been deduced, *barrow* being synonymous with *fortress* or *hill.* The manor itself would seem to have been identical with the Tolentone of Domesday Book, which was held, in the time of William the Conqueror, by Ranulf, brother of Ilger, whose manorial rights were valued at forty shillings. Still earlier, in the reign of Edward the Confessor, it was occupied by one of his vassals, Edwin. Tollentone, or Tallington Lane, afterwards known as Devil's Lane, and now as Hornsey Road, divided Highbury from St. John's, Clerkenwell. On the east side of this lane formerly stood the original dwelling of the lords, styled in contemporary records *The Lower Place.* As this

D

house had gradually fallen into decay, a new one was built on the high ground to the eastward, and from its position, in relation to the former, the manor is presumed to have derived the name of Highbury. In 1271 the then proprietress, Alice de Barrowe, made over the entire lordship of Highbury and Newington to the Priory of St. John of Jerusalem, and henceforward the manor-house appears to have been used as the *refuge*, or country-seat of the priors, until burnt by Wat Tyler and the rebels, in the reign of Richard II. It was a building of considerable beauty, and was constructed of such solid materials, that the incendiaries found some difficulty in demolishing it, and were compelled, it is said, to pull down, by main force, such portions of the walls as the fire failed to consume.

The manor continued in the hands of the priors until the period of the Reformation, when it was granted by Henry VIII. to Thomas, Lord Cromwell, but reverted to the Crown upon his attainder in 1540. It was subsequently bestowed by James I. on his eldest son, Prince Henry. In 1629 Charles I. presented it to Sir Allen Apsley, who sold it in the following year to Thomas Austen. A descendant of the latter, Sir John Austen, alienated it, in 1723, to Thomas Colebrooke; Mr. Colebrooke's son, or grandson, Sir George Colebrooke, having become a bankrupt, his interest in the manor was sold, during 1791, to Mr. Jonathan Eade, of Stoke Newington, and it is still held, we believe, by the representatives of the latter owner.

The first mention of the Barn itself occurs, so far as

we have been able to trace, in 1438, when Sir William Eastfield, Knight of the Bath, and the Lord Mayor for that year, erected conduits in Fleet Street, Aldermanbury, and Cripplegate, the water for which was supplied from Highbury Barn.

The following indenture of a lease—transcribed in modern English—bearing date 1505, has also been preserved:—

" This indenture, made between Sir Thomas Docwra, Prior of the Hospital of St. John of Jerusalem, in England, and his brethren of the same hospital, on the one part, and William Woodmanton, otherwise called William Mantyll, of London, butcher, on the other part, witnesseth that the said Prior, and his brethren, by their whole assent and authority of their chapter, have granted, and let to farm, to the aforesaid William Woodmanton, their grange place, built upon the site of their manor of Highbury, called Highbury Barn, in the county of Middlesex, with a garden and castle hills there, and with two little enclosures, containing, by estimation, five acres, lying upon the north part of the said garden, together with a field, called Snorefield, otherwise Bushfield, in the county aforesaid. Always reserving to the said Prior, and his successors, woods and underwoods, waifs and strays. To have and to hold every part aforesaid except before, except to the aforesaid William Woodmanton, and his assignees, from the feast of St. Michael the Archangel, next following after the date thereof, unto the end and term of twenty-one years then next following, and fully to be ended. Yielding and paying therefor yearly

to the said Prior, and his successors, at the treasury of
their house of Clerkenwell, near London, ten pounds
sterling, at four terms of the year, that is to say, at Christmas, Annunciation of our Lady, Nativity of St. John the
Baptist, and St. Michael the Archangel, by even portions.
And bearing all manner of charges, ordinary and extraordinary, going out of the said grange, garden, enclosures,
and fields, during the said term.   And the said farmer
and his assignees, at their cost, shall repair and maintain
the aforesaid grange place, as in tiling and daubing, and
also shall repair, make, and sustain all manner of hedges
and ditches of the aforesaid garden, enclosures, and
fields, during the said term, and in the end of the same
term, the said grange place, as in tiling and daubing, and
the said enclosures, garden, and fields, as in hedging and
ditching, shall leave sufficiently repaired.   The enclosure
and hedging of Highbury Wood only excepted.   Also it
shall be lawful to the said farmer and his assignees to
stock and dig the aforesaid field, called Snorefield, without impeachment of waste.   And the same field, at the
end of the said term, shall be left well and clean, stocked,
and cleared of briars and bushes growing in the same.
And the aforesaid farmer, and his assignees, by assign-
ment of the officer of the said Prior, and his successors,
shall have, in and of the woods, underwoods, and thorns,
growing there, hedgebote during the said term.   Also it
shall be lawful to the said farmer, and to his assignees,
to have for ingress and egress, with their cattle, the old
way accustomed to and from the said pastures, which
way is specially reserved to the said Prior and his tenants,

in a lease made to William Sharpe, of certain pastures belonging to the said manor of Highbury. And if it chances that the said yearly rent and farm of ten pounds sterling be behindhand, and not paid in part in the whole, after any term of payment before specified, in this indenture, by the space of eleven months, that then it shall be lawful to the said Prior, and his successors, to re-enter into the aforesaid grange, garden, enclosures, and fields. And all the same to enjoy, as in their first estate. This present lease notwithstanding. In witness whereof to one part of these present indentures toward the said William Woodmanton remaining, the said Prior and his brethren have put their convent seal. And to the other part of the same indenture towards the said Prior and his brethren abiding, the said William Woodmanton hath put his seal. Given in the chapter-house of the said Prior and brethren, the twenty-eighth day of June, in the year of our Lord God 1505, and the twentieth year of the reign of King Henry VII."

In a survey of the manor, taken by order of Prince Henry, in 1611, Highbury Barn is depicted as a high building within the castle yard. As years rolled on, the London citizens were in the habit of walking out to Highbury to drink new milk, and eat custards, cakes, and syllabubs, and so gradually the farm grew into a tavern and tea-garden, at first on a very humble scale, but increasing in importance proportionately with its rise in popular favour. The Court-baron of the manor was held here, and in time a large room was added, and handsomely fitted up, for the reception of the company in wet weather. The Highbury Society—of Protestant dissenters—established in 1714, on the death of Queen Anne, celebrated its meetings here as early as, or perhaps earlier than, 1740. The following toast was always given at their annual dinner, in the month of August:—"The glorious 1st of August, with the immortal memory of King William and Queen Mary, not forgetting Corporal John; and a fig for the Bishop of Cork, that bottle-stopper." By Corporal John was meant the great Duke of Marlborough. This society was dissolved in 1833. And during its long-continued,. although not very brilliant, existence, Highbury Barn may at least boast of one most honoured tradition. It shared, with White Conduit House, the distinction of being, at one period of his life, the favourite pleasure-haunt of the poet, Oliver Goldsmith. In the years 1762-4, when the then struggling author was hiding from his creditors, under the wing of Mr. Newberry—of picture-book renown—and composing his immortal *Vicar of Wakefield*, at Canonbury Tower, Goldsmith was often wont to seek distraction—and, possibly, ideas—for his book, in what he would humorously term a "shoemaker's holiday." This would consist in a morning walk by the City Road, and through the fields, to dine at Highbury Barn. "There was *then*," we are told by his friend and fellow-student, Cooke, when writing in the *European Magazine*, for 1793, "a very good ordinary, of two dishes, and a pastry, kept at Highbury Barn, at tenpence per head, including a penny to the waiter; and the company consisted of literary characters, a few Templars, and some citizens who had left off trade ; the whole expenses of the day's *fête* never exceeded a crown, and oftener were from three-and-sixpence to four shillings, for which the party obtained good air and exercise, the example of simple manners, and good conversation." How much of all this could be affirmed, with equal truth, by any one of the visitors to its more splendid rivals; the gardens of Marylebone, Ranelagh, and Vauxhall ?

In the *Gentleman's Magazine* for December, 1785, we find, amongst the obituary of considerable persons : " 17th, Mr. Willoughby, master of the place of public entertainment called Highbury Barn." It was under this proprietor that the bowling-green, trapball-ground, and gardens were first laid out, and both he, and sub·sequently his son, by their persevering industry and excellent arrangements, greatly increased the popularity of the place. In the Crace Collection of " Views of Old London," exhibited in the year 1879, at the South Kensington Museum, there was an engraving of Highbury Barn, described as " The Highbury Assembly House, near Islington, kept by Mr. Willoughby, published 12th September, 1792, by Robert Sayer & Co., Fleet Street, London."

In addition to the Highbury Society, a number of corporate bodies, public charities, and clubs now began to hold their annual gatherings here ; and in 1801, it is recorded that a dinner was dressed for eight hundred persons, all of whom sat down to hot dishes. On this occasion, no less than seventy geese might be seen roasting at one fire. In June, 1808, the Society of Free-

masons, to the number of five hundred, after attending
divine service at Islington Church, dined at the Highbury Tavern, and a similar feasting was repeated in
1810. Nelson, in his *History of Islington*, published in
1811, describes its increasing prosperity, and says that
"the business done at this house, in the summer months,
is equal to, if not beyond, that of any similar concern in
the metropolis or its environs. From the grounds the
prospect is extensive and beautiful; at one end is a
small plantation of hops, which has been for these few
years past cultivated by Mr. Willoughby, who has lately
erected a very convenient ale and table-beer brewery on
the premises. An assembly is likewise established here,
which is supported by the subscriptions of the neighbouring inhabitants, who meet together in the great room
once a month during the seasons of winter and spring.
In a field adjoining the gardens is a butt for the
exercise of ball-firing, similar to the one at Canonbury."

On the 4th of June, 1818, the first annual celebra-
tion of the British and Foreign School Society was held
here, and presided over by the Duke of Sussex. Four
thousand children—three hundred of whom were Jews,—
walked in procession, and were examined in the grounds.
In Leigh's *New Picture of London*, for 1825, Highbury
Barn is described as "a tavern and tea-gardens, which
are very much frequented, particularly during the summer." In 1835 the long room contained two pictures,
which had formerly hung in the Duke of Northumber-
land's gallery at Sion House. One of these was the
" full-length portrait of a lady dressed in the old style,

the other represented " Venus lamenting over the dead body of Adonis."

From the Willoughbys the concern passed to Mr. John Hinton, in whose hands, and those of his son, Mr. Archibald Hinton, it remained down to the year 1860. Under the two Hintons, Highbury Barn continued to preserve most of its old characteristics, and was long the favoured place of meeting for clubs and large societies. The Licensed Victuallers, for instance, held their annual dinner there, in 1841, which was attended by as many as three thousand guests. Musical performances and pyrotechnic displays were in time added to the more primitive attractions, but these were always concluded by a comparatively early hour. The element of *fastness*, which prevailed more and more as time slipped by, at places like Vauxhall and Cremorne, was conspicuous only by its absence here. Appealing like the Surrey Gardens— another place of amusement, now also defunct—more exclusively to the middle and tradesman class, Highbury Barn might be beneath the notice of the gilded youth of that day ; but it was, at any rate, always thoroughly *respectable.*

Passing over a few years, we next read of assemblies for dancing as being held in the large room during the winter months of 1849-50, and of a Licensed Victuallers' anniversary dinner, in May, 1851. This was presided over by Mr. Samuel Whitbread, M.P., and the exceptionally large sum of 4044*l.* was collected after dinner in aid of the Society's funds. A musical festival was given in June, 1852 ; and amongst the Societies who held their *fêtes* in 1853, were the Tinplate-Workers, the Cork-Cutters, the United Patriots, Waltonians, and News-vendors.

Whether owing to a diminution of popular favour, or from some other cause, we know not, but in the next year, 1854, the place began to assume rather a different aspect. At any rate, the old routine did not seem to satisfy the proprietor. So the band of the Grenadier Guards was engaged, and dancing introduced every evening, from seven till half-past ten. The licence for dancing was, however, refused by the magistrates at the end of the season. This year was also memorable for a balloon ascent, made by the veteran aeronaut Green, on the evening of the 10th of July. A panorama of Constantinople was exhibited in the long room, in 1855; and to evade the licence, dancing now took place under the auspices of a number of subscribers, who styled themselves the Highbury Club. The much-contested licence was at length granted in October, 1856, and from this date the class of frequenters gradually changed, until at length the time-honoured tea-garden, "the pride of merrie Islington," became finally transformed into a species of North London Cremorne. A carnival ball was given on Easter Monday, 1859, when one thousand presents were distributed amongst the visitors. The celebrated comic vocalist, Mackney, sang at Mr. Hinton's benefit in September, 1860. The proprietor retired to Anerley Gardens at the end of this year, having relinquished his lease to Mr. Edward Giovanelli, who assumed the reins of management on Whit Monday,

May 21st, 1861. A new music hall was constructed in 1862, in which concerts were given, with Miss Rebecca Isaacs and Mr. Vernon Rigby as the leading singers. That most graceful of gymnasts, Leotard, was also engaged for the whole of the season. The night of Thursday, the 16th of August, witnessed a terrible accident to a woman, professionally known as "The Female Blondin," but whose real name was Selina Young, and who, whilst walking on a tight-rope, at an elevation of sixty feet from the ground, and balancing herself by a pole loaded with fireworks in full play, fell, and was crippled for life. A once favourite ballet, *The Beauty of Ghent*, was represented in 1863, and Professor Pepper's "Ghost" also formed a great attraction in this year, scenes from *Hamlet* and *Der Freischütz* being expressly mounted for its display. Promenade Concerts were given in the winter of 1864.

Many alterations and improvements in the gardens were effected in 1865, and the music-hall was converted into a theatre, the Alexandra, which was opened on the 20th of May, with a burlesque on the opera of *Ernani*, by the well-known author, William Brough ; the burlesque was preceded by a new farce, bearing the eccentric title of *Worrybury's Whims*. These pieces were supported by Miss Rachel Sanger, Mrs. Caulfield, Mr. Danvers, and Mr. J. G. Taylor. Mr. Giovanelli himself also played Wormwood, in *The Lottery Ticket*, and a pantomime, on the well-worn subject of *Bluebeard*, was produced at Christmas. The qualifications of the lessee as an actor were certainly various, seeing that within the next two or three years he appeared successively in such parts as Jem Baggs, in *The Wandering Minstrel*, Jacob Earwig, in *Boots at the Swan*, as clown in the revived and once famous pantomime of *Mother Goose*, and as Mawworm in Bickerstaffe's comedy of *The Hypocrite*.

The theatre now divided attention with the gardens, and was worked for some time with energy and success; but other amusements were not neglected. Benefit societies and bean-feasts continued to be held, and the out-of-door attractions were set forth with as much prominence as ever. Blondin, the equilibrist, was engaged in the summer of 1868, and another celebrity, Natator, the man frog, in 1869. During this latter year, also, a curiosity, or monstrosity, of a former generation, The Siamese Twins, on their return, after an interval of many years, to England, were exhibited here. The art of puffery would really seem to have reached its extreme limit in the advertisements at this date. Vauxhall, in its palmy days, had been wont to glory in an illumination of *twenty thousand extra* lamps; Highbury Barn now boasted of *half a million!* But neither these, nor the exertions —which, however misdirected, were at any rate great—of Mr. Giovanelli, could long uphold the credit of a place the respectability of which had completely disappeared. The drunken and riotous orgies entailed by the late hour up to which the gardens were kept open, had made them a nuisance to the inhabitants of this rapidly increasing suburb. The opposition to the annual licence became more and more general, until at length matters were brought to a crisis by the ill-advised exhibition of the Colonna troupe of dancers, in June, 1870. This step proved fatal. The local authorities now interfered, the licence was cancelled, and the lessee, who, by his own showing, had expended upwards of thirty-five thousand pounds upon the property, withdrew from the scene, at the end of the summer—a ruined man.

In 1871 yet one more effort was made for Highbury Barn, the speculator this time happening to be no other than the ubiquitous Mr. E. T. Smith, who in his time had governed more places of public entertainment in London than any other individual, since or before, and who now made shift to carry it on, with most of the old amusements, minus the objectionable dancing. On the 27th of June, in this year, a race of five hundred pigeons took place; the birds been let loose at noon, arrived at Courtrai, in Belgium, as specified by a telegram, at half-past three, during the afternoon. A similar race, on a more extended scale, occurred at Sydenham in the same month; but this one, as an event in the history of Highbury Barn, deserves to be recorded here. Mr. E. T. Smith, however, proved powerless to restore its fallen fortunes; and, notwithstanding his quaintly-piteous protest that, in order to meet the popular prejudice, *five hundred bakers*, and their *five hundred wives*, had been forbidden to dance, after their annual dinner, held in the summer, the renewal of his lease was inexorably refused in the following October.

From this date Highbury Barn remained shut up entirely, seeing that no other tenant could be found endowed with sufficient hardihood to bid for a place over the gates of which *Ichabod* might indeed have been long since most fitly written up. On the occasion of a recent visit, we found the entrance—which had formerly some pretension to architectural merit—half demolished, and the intervening gaps filled in with common wooden hoardings. The flower beds were choked with grass and weeds. The nightshade flourished in rank luxuriance around the crumbling and dismantled orchestra. The once elegant decorations of the Alexandra Theatre were all but obliterated by damp and mildew, whilst the windows of the " vast and unequalled " ball-room—a room, by the way, of really noble proportions—were completely destitute of glass. Two of the five acres, set forth in Docwra's indenture, had been already built upon. The remaining three formed, indeed, but a sorry monument of departed folly. And sad though it must ever be to witness the removal of an ancient land-mark, we cannot but hope that, continuing merely under such conditions as these, Highbury Barn may speedily be improved off the face of the earth altogether. For though the venerable Tower of Canonbury, the shelter of Oliver Goldsmith during the fruition of his choicest literary toils, may well rear its head erect, and bid defiance to a time which can cast no taint upon the history of its past ; the poor old Barn, the scene of his innocent hours of recreation, now exists merely as a tawdry, dreary, and—to tell the honest truth—a most disreputable-looking ruin, in the midst of modern, smiling, prosperous Highbury.

THE DRAMA IN NORTON-FOLGATE.

A *very* MINOR RECORD.

THE abolition of patent rights, hitherto confined exclusively to the two large houses—Drury Lane and Covent Garden—and the consequent diffusion of dramatic enterprise, called into existence during the second quarter of the present century a number of new theatres in every part of the metropolis.   One of these—the City of London Theatre, in Bishopsgate Street, Norton-Folgate—although owing to a remote situation, and other causes, it scarcely ever achieved *Fame*, and never *Fashion*, maintained, nevertheless, for a period of many years, a certain position and popularity of its own, which may fairly entitle it to a niche in the archives of the London stage. The house in Norton-Folgate, however, should not be confounded with another City Theatre, opened a few years earlier in Grub Street—now Milton Street.[1]   This City

---

[1] The New City Subscription Theatre, Milton Street, Fore Street, was constructed by Mr. Bedford, and first opened to the public at Easter, 1831. The lessee was Mr. John Kemble Chapman, who had married Miss Anne Tree, sister of the more famous Miss Ellen Tree—afterwards Mrs. Charles Kean. The introductory entertainments were of a light description, but were supported by the talents of Mr. John

Theatre, after a brief career, had succumbed to circum-

Reeve, Mr. Macarthy, Mrs. Fitzwilliam, and Miss Pincott, in addition to the lessee, and his clever wife. Although no licence had been obtained for the performance of the legiti- mate drama, an engagement was effected with Edmund Kean, who appeared on the 23rd of May, and during his visit played Shylock, King Lear, Othello, Sir Edward Mortimer, and Sir Giles Overreach. This engagement remains as the one great tradition of the little theatre in Milton Street, which neverthe- less, from time to time, could boast of some very good names in its bills. T. P. Cooke played William in *Black-Eyed Susan*, to the Gnatbrain of J. B. Buckstone, in June, and in August James Vining and Miss Ellen Tree were secured, the latter playing Eily O'Connor, in a dramatized version of Gerald Griffin's novel, " The Collegians," the plot of which was long afterwards—at the Adelphi, in 1860—turned to such brilliant account, by Dion Boucicault, in *The Colleen Bawn.* Tyrone Power was the " star " in August, supported by Miss Ellen Tree, Miss Apjohn—better remembered as Mrs. Frank Matthews—Mr. James Vining, and Mr. Shepherd. Still later in the year, Mr. and Mrs. Davidge, and Mrs. Selby were to be seen, in *Guy Mannering* and *Victorine.* Davidge assumed the management in January, 1832, and engaged Miss Smithson—who subsequently became the wife of Hector Berlioz—as his leading actress. Mr. Benjamin Webster made his first essay in theatrical management, at the City, at Easter in this year, and engaged George Bennett, Oxberry, and Mrs. Waylett. Mr. Chapman resumed the direction at Christmas, with a new piece, *The Gentleman in Black*, from the pen of Leman Rede. The same author's dramas, *The Rake's Progress*, and *Five Degrees of Crime*, were then pro- duced with success. Mr. Butler, of Covent Garden, played legitimate first lead in July, 1833, and John Reeve was also engaged, with the favourite comedian, Mr. T. Green, and the celebrated clown, Paulo. The dramatist Moncrieff was the

stances, and reverted to its original condition—a conventicle—a short time before our history opens.

The erection of the new house was commenced as early as October, 1834, but owing to a difficulty about the licence, or, more probably, want of money, it did not open until Monday, March 27, 1837. It was built by Beazley, the most celebrated theatrical architect of his time, and whose work can still be seen in Drury Lane, the St. James's, and Lyceum. For massive richness of decoration, and harmony of outline, these three houses may contrast favourably with the majority of our modern theatres, in which general effect is for the most part sacrificed to a practical anxiety for conveniently seating as many spectators as possible. The artists of to-day have undoubtedly improved upon their predecessors as regards comfort; but they are as far behind them in the symmetry and completeness of their work. If the architecture of our older playhouses occasionally erred on the side of heaviness, that of the present is too often conspicuous for its nakedness and meagre ornamentation. The new Haymarket Theatre, opened at the beginning of last year, is, indeed, a model of beauty and luxurious accommodation; but the Haymarket is unhappily an exception to the prevailing rule of theatrical construction in London.

The prominent features of the new theatre, which

next manager, and gave a series of his own dramas, but from this time the performances call for no special notice, being mostly of a very inferior kind, although the names of Oxberry and Mrs. H. P. Grattan were to be met with occasionally in the announcements for 1835. After that year the City Theatre disappears altogether.

E

opened, as we have before said, on Easter Monday, 1837, were an elegant Corinthian *façade*, which still remains, and a small, but very prettily decorated, interior. The lessee was Mr. Cockerton, formerly connected with the Olympic, and the opening piece was a dramatic version, by Mr. Edward Stirling, of Dickens' then new and universally popular *Pickwick*, with Mr. Macarthy as Jingle, and two other old favourites, Wilkinson and W. H. Williams, in the part of Sam Weller and the title *rôle*. Mrs. Emden, whose husband was stage-manager—Miss Rivers, and Mr. Wrench, were also in the company. The scenery, by Mr. Charles Marshall, afterwards scenic artist at Her Majesty's Theatre, in the days of Lumley, was greatly admired. The musical arrangements were under the direction of Mr. J. H. Tully, subsequently, for a long period, the popular conductor of the orchestra at Drury Lane, and the entire performance was pronounced a decided success. Mr. George Bennett played Hamlet on Wednesday, the 3rd of May, for the benefit of the distressed weavers, and during the same month a troupe of Bedouin Arabs were added to the other, and more legitimate, attractions. On Monday, the 26th of June, the old musical drama, *The Lord of the Manor*, was given, for the benefit of Mr. Cockerton.

The house re-opened for the winter on Monday, the 16th of October, under the direction of the same lessee, with the addition of Mr. Edward Stirling as stage-manager. A fortnight afterwards, Mrs. Honey, one of the most beautiful and popular actresses of the day, appeared in *Don Juan*. Miss Pincott, afterwards Mrs. Alfred Wigan, and the celebrated low comedian, Vale, were also en-

gaged. Of Vale, when at the Surrey Theatre, a contemporary critic [2] writes, " Mr. Vale has a most enviable hold on
the Surrey audience; he enters—they laugh, he looks—
they laugh, he speaks—they laugh, he moves—they laugh,
he stops—they laugh, he goes off—they laugh ; in short,
do what he may—they laugh, and even sometimes do what
he may not—they laugh. If we were to write a piece for
the Surrey Theatre, we should make but one stipulation
—' let Mr. Vale play in it.' The audience would be satis-
fied, and so should we." Needless to add how important
such an acquisition would be, to a young and struggling
house like the New City. On Boxing-night Mrs. Honey
assumed the management, beginning her reign with a
spectacle, *The Page of Palermo,* and a pantomime, *Will
o' the Wisp,* in which Harry Boleno, the Messrs. Deulin,
Miss Gilbert and Miss Pincott, all appeared.

In the early months of 1838 the plays successively
performed were *Clari, the Maid of Milan, The Beulah
Spa, Hush Money, The Rent Day,* and *The Dream at Sea*
—with Mrs. Honey as Biddy Nutts.[3] Mrs. Honey gave
up the theatre at Easter to Osbaldiston—a well-known
actor of melodrama, and theatrical manager in his day—
who opened with a new play, *Windsor Castle in the Olden
Time,* in which he played the leading character, supported
by Freer, Simpson, Mrs. Edwin Yarnold, and Miss Vincent. Osbaldiston managed the house for three years,
during which Miss Vincent, then in the pride of her

---

[2] *Athenæum,* March 9, 1833.
[3] The leading actor of Mrs. Honey's company was Mr. T.
Green, familiarly known as " Gentleman " Green.

youthful beauty and talent, formed the leading attraction. This was an actress who, under other conditions, might have gone far in the highest walks of her art. Fate, and Mr. Osbaldiston, however, ruled it differently, and as " the only heroine of domestic tragedy," Miss Vincent was content to shine, at theatres of a very inferior grade to those on the boards of which she might otherwise have occupied a leading position. On Saturday, the 18th of June, 1839, there was a benefit for the General Theatrical Fund, when T. P. Cooke appeared as William in *Black-Eyed Susan*. Mrs. Waylett, Mr. and Mrs. Keeley, Hammond, and Strickland all lent their aid on this occasion. Mr. and Mrs. Frank Matthews, Oxberry, and Mrs. Honey produced some of Madame Vestris' Olympic pieces in the July of this year. The pantomimes, under Mr. Osbaldiston's reign, were written by Nelson Lee. The character of the City Theatre, however, gradually sank to a very low ebb, as may be guessed from the titles of some of the dramas. *The Bandit's Bride, The Patriot's Doom, The Pool of the Drowned, The Miser's Grave, The Tailor's Dream, Sweet Poll of Horsleydown, Jack Sheppard*, and *Sixteen-String Jack ;* such was the fare offered in the year 1840 to the respectable inhabitants of Norton-Folgate. Another melodrama, *Mary Clifford*, seems to have been of a superior order, and had a run of between sixty and seventy nights.

At Easter, 1841, Osbaldiston and Miss Vincent removed to the Victoria, leaving the field once more clear for Mr. Cockerton, who now renewed his experiment in conjunction with Mr. Shepherd—in years to come the successful manager of the Surrey. *Inez di Castro* was the first novelty of the new season, with Mrs. Honey and Miss Emmeline Montague, who afterwards became Mrs. Compton. Carter's lions were exhibited in May, in a spectacular piece, *The Lion of the Desert.* Passing on to the following year, we find Mr. Charles Dillon playing at Easter, and the famous clown, Tom Matthews, at Whitsuntide. Shakspeare's *Romeo and Juliet* was given on Monday, the 17th of October, with Charles Dillon and Miss E. Montague in the leading parts. Mrs. Honey also was still in the company, but the exhibition of a notorious individual, Alice Lowe, "the victim of unmerited persecution," who had recently figured in the Law Courts, testifies to the small account in which the respectability of his theatre was held by the proprietor. A very good pantomime, *Harlequin and the One-Eyed Blacksmith*, written by Nelson Lee, was produced on Boxing-night, with Milano as Harlequin, Blanchard as Clown, and Miss Cushnie, Columbine.

The Tower of Nêsle, The Miller and his Men, and *Black-Eyed Susan,* respectively, ushered in the pantomime during January, 1843. Mr. Dillon returned in the following month, and played, with Mrs. Yarnold, in *Othello, Romeo and Juliet,* and *Richard the Third,* as well as in Tobin's comedy of *The Honeymoon,* and "Monk" Lewis's once popular melodrama, *The Castle Spectre.* Mr. Elton, another very striking actor, was here in March, appearing in *Julius Cæsar,* and Massinger's fine tragedy, *A New Way to Pay Old Debts.* Mrs. Honey also played, for the last time in public, a few nights before her pre-

mature death, towards the end of this month.   Mr. C. S.
James, of the Tottenham Street Theatre—now the Prince
of Wales's—assumed the management at Easter, with
Miss Kate Howard as leading actress, and Mr. O. Smith
from the Adelphi.   A portion of Macready's company at
Drury Lane, including Mr. George Bennett, Mr. Ryder,
Mrs. W. West, and Miss Fortescue, gave a series of
"legitimate" performances in July, but for the remainder
of the year drama of a very low type was the prevailing
rule.   Mr. Denvil, the original representative of Lord
Byron's *Manfred*, afforded some relief to the state of
things early in the ensuing year, by playing in the *Merchant of Venice, Pizarro*, and other legitimate plays.   These
were succeeded in March by the equestrian spectacle of
Mazeppa, and at Easter the celebrated pantomimist,
Wieland, Mr. Wilsone, Mrs. Frank Matthews, and Miss
Emma Stanley were engaged.

During the autumn of 1844, in emulation, it may be
presumed, of the excellent example lately set—and with
such good results—by Phelps and Mrs. Warner at Sadler's
Wells, an effort was made to improve the style of performances, and generally to impart a higher tone.
Accordingly the house was re-decorated, and opened on
Monday, the 7th of October, under the lesseeship of Mr.
Wilsone, and the stage-direction of that very admirable
actress, Mrs. Walter Lacy, whose name figured promi-
nently in all the announcements.   Sheridan's *School for
Scandal* was given by a fair, though incomplete company,
comprising, however, the good names of Messrs. James
Browne, Robert Roxby, George Wild, B. Rogers, Mrs.

Tayleure, Miss Daly, and the new manageress, who, of course, played Lady Teazle, and, in the course of the evening, delivered the following address, from the pen of Albert Smith :—

" Accustomed as I am to public speaking,
 Yet I must own, in thus your favours seeking,
 I trembling come before you, on reflection,
 That all is now under my sole direction.
 But should you find for blame the least pretence,
 Pray pardon me, for 'tis my first offence.

" The Drama long has wander'd up and down,
 Spurn'd in the country—starved to death in town ;
 Received into no Union ; and at last,
 Without a bit of food, was *breaking fast,*
 We come to offer her indoor relief,
 And though of all, our house is not the chief ;
 Shakspere himself, I'm sure, would rather rest
 Free in the City, than at Court *compressed.*

" While music, painting, wit, its worth enhance,
 In our Art-Union will you take a chance ?
 You need not be afraid ; for though of late
 All play has been abolish'd by the State,
 Yet, in this instance, we are glad to say,
 No ' Qui Tam ' actions can affect our play ;
 And still we hope your patronage to gain,
 Each piece produced will have a ' running reign.'
 Our novelty with worth shall be combined,
 And though our subjects are most hard to find,
 Yet on the Drama's ground—the area's wide—
 We'll try and seek some ' plot unoccupied.'

" One moment to our ballet let me turn,
 Train'd for our new campaign by Oscar Byrne,

Who, with his bright array of female charms,
Is trusting more to legs than feats of arms,
Two[4] of the *corps* are strangers in the land,
But with right energy have join'd our band.
Pray make them feel that nothing ere should be
'Twixt France and merry England, but the sea.

" Events and changes latterly have shown
Women can make each province quite their own.
The Salic law in theatres is repeal'd,
And women now alone the sceptres wield.
Think not the undertaking new or strange,
In opening this night *our* new Exchange ;
But rally round our house, and prove at least
There yet remains some wisdom in the East."

The play was very well mounted, and the *divertissement* which followed, and to which allusion was made in the introductory speech, was admirably got up by Oscar Byrne, the best English ballet-master of his day. Sheridan's comedy was followed, at a short interval, by Mrs. Cowley's *Belle's Stratagem*, and Holcroft's *Road to Ruin*, but either this class of entertainment was too refined for the denizens of the far East, or else funds were wanting for its proper establishment there. At any rate the new venture did not thrive, and eventually came to a sudden, and regrettable termination, within a month from the date of its commencement.

The house was consequently "to let" at the very height of the winter season, but the irrepressible Mr. Cockerton speedily came, once more, to the front, and

---

[4] Mdlles. Louise, and Adèle, announced as of Her Majesty's Theatre, and the San Carlo-Naples. Both dancers, later, became established favourites, at the smaller London theatres.

reopened it on Boxing-night, with Sheridan's *Pizarro*, and a pantomime, bearing the attractive title, *The Gnomes of the Golden Caves*. His stage-manager was now Mr. Denvil, who reappeared on the 30th of December as Shylock.

The American dwarf, Tom Thumb, was exhibited at the City of London, during the first week in January, 1845, and a tragedian of some merit, Mr. Hudson Kirby, from the same country, also had an engagement. Mr. and Miss Vandenhoff were playing here, during the month of April, in *As You Like It*. The next lessee was Mr. Robert Honner, who opened it for the winter season on Monday, the 27th of October, with a drama, *Pauline*, which later playgoers may recollect as a favourite after-piece at the Princess's Theatre, in the time of Charles Kean. Mr. Ryder had a benefit, on Monday, the 22nd of December, when *Virginius* was played. The performances, as a whole, were greatly improved this winter. The well-known harlequin, Bologna, appeared in the pantomime, *King Lud of Ludgate*, at Christmas.

One of the many versions of Dickens' charming tale, *The Cricket on the Hearth*, was brought out in January, 1846, with Mrs. Honner, a pretty and clever actress, as Dot, and the manager as Caleb Plummer. Hughes's performing elephants were to be seen in February, and Lovell's fine play, *Love's Sacrifice*, was acted on Monday, the 16th of March, with Mrs. Honner as Margaret Elmore. Throughout this month, the legitimate drama was largely drawn upon. The favourite Adelphi drama, *Victorine*, was the attraction for the opening of the winter season on Monday, the 31st of August, with Mrs. Honner, Messrs Lyon, and H. T. Craven, the latter of whom subsequently rose to eminence. A Mr. Charles Mason, related, on his mother's side, to the Kembles, next appeared in *Othello*, *Hamlet*, and Byron's *Werner*. In October the lessee started the innovation of a threepenny gallery, and this, if profitable for the time, had, as introducing a lower class of visitors, a most injurious effect upon the character of the house. A new melodrama, *The Black Doctor*, was brought out on Monday, the 9th of November, and on Boxing-night, that excellent clown, Paul Herring, formed the mainstay of the pantomime, *He with the Hump*. A version of Dickens' *Battle of Life*, with Mrs. Honner as Clemency Newcombe, was the next novelty in January, 1847, and Mr. J. R. Scott starred as leading tragedian. Nothing of interest seems to have occurred during the summer months, and the next noticeable event was the production, early in October, of a drama, founded upon Cruikshank's series of illustrations, *The Bottle*. This was extremely well acted by Mrs. Honner, Mrs. Griffiths, Messrs Robert Honner, Lyon, E. F. Savile, Ersser Jones, and H. T. Craven. On Boxing-night a pantomime, *The Old Woman tossed in a Blanket*, by the well-known author, T. W. Moncrieff, formed the concluding event of the year 1847.

In the summer of 1848, Mr. Honner having become bankrupt, the City was under the provisional management of Mr. E. F. Savile, who revived the old comedy, *A Cure for the Heartache*, for his benefit, on Saturday, the 28th of August. On Saturday, the 30th of September, it was re-opened by Mr. Nelson Lee, in conjunction with Mr. J. Johnson, and to these gentlemen belonged the uncommon

merit of conducting the City of London Theatre for a
term extending over many years, not only with credit
and respectability, but with pecuniary results highly satis-
factory to themselves. In fact, they were the only managers
who ever really made it pay. Their plan was to carry on
the theatre themselves in the winter, and to sub-let it during
the summer months, thus keeping open house for the whole
year, with the exception of such time as was requisite for
cleaning, re-decoration, and repairs. This system has since
been very generally adopted elsewhere, though not always
with like results. The remarkable excellence of Mr.
Nelson Lee's pantomimes was another feature which
served to bring the house into notice, whilst, in other
portions of the year, although the lessees were shrewd
enough to measure the requirements of their audiences,
and to provide them with the fare which they seemed to
prefer, they made, in the course of time, many and praiseworthy efforts to cultivate and improve their taste. Mr.
Nelson Lee's first pantomime, under his own management,
was entitled, *War, Love, and Peace*, and proved highly
successful. Mr. Savile was again sub-tenant, for the
summer months of 1849, and engaged that first of all
transpontine favourites, Mr. N. T. Hicks - the " Brayvo
'Icks " of the Victoria gallery—for first lead. The winter
season, which began early in October, was marked by the
production of *The Prophet*, being a dramatic version of
Meyerbeer's latest opera. The pantomime bore the
whimsical title of *Pens, Ink, and Paper*. Mr. Nelson
Lee had a benefit on Wednesday, the 27th of February,
and Mr Johnson on Tuesday, the 16th of April, 1850.

On the latter occasion Mr. Rayner appeared in *King Lear.*
Mr. Savile, as usual, directed the summer season, and
when the lessees returned for the winter, a play founded
on Verdi's opera of *Nabucco,* entitled *Anato, King of
Assyria,* was produced.   The Christmas pantomime,
Knife, Fork, and Spoon — an unusually good one—served
to introduced a new clown, Mr. George Parry, to the
London public.

In January, 1851, a version of *Belphegor the Mountebank* was produced with success, and at Easter a drama,
the subject of which was musically treated by the composer, Vincent Wallace, some ten years later at the
Opera-house in the Haymarket—*The Amber Witch.* At
Whitsuntide we read of an oriental spectacle, with the
sonorous title, *Zenobia, Queen of Palmyra.* A new stage
had been laid down, before the winter season, which
began at Michaelmas, with a drama, *King Liberty.*
Another, *The Slaves of London,* first saw the light in the
middle of October.   On Monday, the 10th of November,
Mr. James Anderson, who had suffered, it is to be feared,
very considerably in purse by his spirited efforts to
restore legitimacy to the arena of Drury Lane, entered
upon an engagement at the City, and opened with
Hamlet.   Mrs. Lovell's classical play of *Ingomar,* and
Schiller's *Robbers* followed.   *Money* was also most carefully produced, during the last week of Mr. Anderson's
visit, which terminated with credit and profit to the
actor and his managers alike, on Saturday, December 23.
On Boxing-night a great success was won for the new
and very clever pantomime, *Oliver Cromwell,* a scene

from which was engraved for the *Illustrated London News ;* a rare distinction in days when illustrated journals and magazines were not—as now—innumerable.

Mr. N. T. Hicks was again engaged, in January, and Mr. Charles Pitt, after a long absence from the metropolitan boards, appeared as Lear, on Monday, the 15th of March, 1852. A version of *The Corsican Brothers*, for Mr. Pitt, Mr. N. T. Hicks, and Mrs. Henry Vining, followed on the 22nd of the same month, and at Easter the tragedy of *Gisippus, or the Forgotten Friend*, was produced. This tragedy was written by Mr. Gerald Griffin—better known as the author of a very popular novel, *The Collegians*. It was originally produced, at Drury Lane, in 1842, when that theatre was under the management of Macready. *Gisippus* would appear to have been more remarkable for the fluency and ingenuity of the writing than for any dramatic vigour. Its revival, however, was an enterprising step on the part of the lessees, and the result was successful. Mr. Pitt's engagement, which, like that of Mr. Anderson, had considerably increased the reputation of the house, came to a conclusion on Saturday, the 12th of June. The City of London reopened for the winter, at the beginning of October, with Mr. N. T. Hicks, in a drama, *The Emigrant's Progress*. This was quickly followed by the reappearance of Mr. James Anderson, whose present engagement extended up to Christmas, and included an event of more than common interest in the production of a new five-act drama of unusual merit, by a hitherto unknown writer, Mr. John Wilkins. This play, entitled *Civilisation*, was not only brilliantly successful at the time, but would seem to have marked a new era in theatrical progress, inasmuch as its ultimate career went to prove that original works might be produced at theatres removed by their locality from all fashionable influence, and yet, by their own intrinsic excellence, win public recognition and general acceptance elsewhere.

The scene of this play is laid in France, during the reign of Louis XIV., and the story turns upon the adventures of an orphan, born of French *émigrés* in North America, and reared by some Indians of the Huron district. Arrived at manhood, he had fought with his tribe against the English, and being taken captive, is brought to England, from whence in the year 1689 he escapes to St. Malo, in Brittany. The play opens at this point. The supposed Huron, in his wild and uncultured state, is sadly perplexed by what he now everywhere hears described as " civilization." A priest, the Abbé Gabriel, endeavours to enlighten him, but his keen perception detects on every side the hollow pretences, the sophistry, and treachery of civilized mankind, and he looks upon such civilization with contempt. A young girl, Hortense, however, by the example of her pure and gentle nature, shows him that there is a better side to human nature. He wins her heart, and, becoming a Christian, is baptized by the name of Hercule. He has a rival unfortunately in a courtier, Lascelles, who has recourse to a variety of artifices to prevent their union, and succeeds in this, by the discovery that as Hortense had stood sponsor at the baptism of Hercule, such a marriage would be illegal. But having successfully defended St. Malo against an attack by the English, Hercule now determines to go to Paris, and in an interview with the king, to urge this service as a claim for the hand of Hortense.   He reaches Paris, and even penetrates to Versailles, but is denied access to the presence of Louis, is falsely arrested as an English spy, and finally lodged in the Bastille, where naturally he moralizes with unmixed bitterness on the boasted civilization of Europe. Later on, the king becomes acquainted with the sad story, obtains personal proof of the integrity of Hercule, and not only releases, but gives him a distinguished place at court.   A dispensation for his marriage is moreover procured from Rome, and all now promises well, when Lascelles again intrigues, and obtains from one Victor Le Bel, the secretary of the Abbé Gabriel, what he believes to be the deed of dispensation.   Armed with this, Lascelles forthwith interposes to prevent the marriage, and in a very dramatic scene, tears up the document in the presence of Hercule, Hortense, and the others.   At this critical moment Le Bel suddenly steps forward with the genuine letter.   The troubles of the lovers are at an end, Lascelles is summarily consigned to the Bastille, and with the following noble lines—

> " To hope
> Against despair—to trust against suspicion—
> To feel that woman, and her angel love,
> Are the true rectifiers of the world ;
> And that to her, and her alone, we owe
> The charm that makes our ruggedness a garden.
> Yes, hand in hand must Truth and Honour walk,
> With Woman for the guide !   That's—Civilization ! "

delivered by Hercule, the curtain fell upon a thoroughly well-deserved and an emphatically-pronounced success. The spirit which Mr. Anderson infused into the powerfully drawn character of Hercule, whether struggling with oppression or satirizing the follies of the world, was in the highest degree effective, and his excellent elocution was incessantly greeted with loud and repeated acclamations. He found an admirable foil in the Lascelles of Mr. Hicks, who, not for the first time, showed himself to be the very prince of melodramatic villains. *Civilization* drew very large houses for several weeks, and was followed by a highly meritorious revival of John Fletcher's comedy, *The Elder Brother*, with which Mr. Anderson's second engagement terminated. Mr. Lee's pantomime, for this Christmas, bore the dazzling title of *King Emerald*.

A dramatic version of *Uncle Tom's Cabin*, with Mr. N. T. Hicks, was the first event of 1853, followed, at the end of February, by the re-engagement of Mr. Charles Pitt, for whom " a new tragedy, by the author of *Civilization*," was produced soon after Easter. This was a revision, under a new title, of Mr. Wilkins' earlier drama, *Zenobia.* The interest of the plot of *The Egyptian* arises from the long-continued strife between the Roman and Palmyrene armies, the former of whom are besieging the city. The troops of Zenobia are commanded by Antiochus, a Parthian, who, turning traitor, incurs the wrath of an Egyptian, Zabdas, whose hatred is accentuated by the knowledge that the Parthian is endeavouring to supplant him, in the affections of the Princess Julia, the daughter of Zenobia, and who is herself attached to a young Roman lord, Gracchus. Zabdas encounters innumerable dangers on behalf of Julia, slays Antiochus, in single combat, and finally loses his life, at the moment of rescuing the Princess, and her Roman lover, from destruction. Mr. Charles Pitt, always a very good actor, was quite at his best, in the part of Zabdas, nor was Mr. N. T. Hicks seen to less advantage, as Antiochus. Scarcely so fine a play as *Civilization*, owing to an occasional inflation of style, *The Egyptian* proved, nevertheless, to have more than average merit, and certainly detracted nothing from the credit of the young writer, whose newly-acquired fame was, however, brought to a premature close by death,[4] on Monday, the 29th of August in this year, and before he had been able to reap any substantial gain, from his recent literary successes. So far, indeed, was this from being the case, that Mr. Wilkins had been thankful to obtain an engagement, to act in small parts, at Sadler's Wells Theatre, where he had played Hecate in *Macbeth*, only two nights before his decease. For John Wilkins had been simply "a poor player," ready to eke out his slender salary, by undertaking the humble duties of authorship, at a minor theatre; that is to say, he had to write, alter, adapt, or rearrange, for a stipend of about thirty-five shillings a week, any sort of dramatic handiwork set to him by his manager. The position has been graphically drawn by Albert Smith, in his *Adventures of the Scattergood Family*. That Mr. Wilkins could rise superior to such a lot, and compose plays like *Civilization* and *The Egyptian*, is,

[4] In his twenty-seventh year.

F

after all, but one more proof that genius, however tram-
melled, must, sooner or later, always come to the front.
Yet that a career of such rich promise should have been
thus early cut off, would be indeed sad to reflect upon,
could we not also turn to the reverse of the picture,
and call up, in imagination, the toil, and drudgery, of
that daily life, and the weary task so soon—because so
well—fulfilled, and—the exchange.

Mr. John Wilkins left, at his death, several plays,
hitherto unacted, one of which, founded on Douglas
Jerrold's story, *St. James' and St. Giles'*, was mounted for
Mr. Rayner in October. Mr. Davenport and Miss
Fanny Vining then "starred," amongst other plays, in an
American tragedy, *Jack Cade*, till Christmas, when Paul
Herring appeared, as clown, in the pantomime of *The
Ocean Queen*. A version, by Mr. Edward Stirling, of
La Prière des Naufrages, already so popular at the
Adelphi, and here entitled *The Struggle for Gold*, was
successfully produced in the middle of January, 1854,
and another play from the portfolio of Mr. Wilkins,
Charity's Love, early in March, for Mr. Davenport and
Miss Vining. "That astounding favourite" (*vide* bills),
Mr. Charles Pitt, returned at Easter and played Bottom,
in a creditably got-up revival of Shakspeare's *Midsummer
Night's Dream*, on Whit Monday, the 5th of June. The
American actor, Mr. Buchanan, was here in August, and
Mr. Gustavus Brooke played a round of Shakspearian, and
other characters, to immense audiences, in October and
November. Mr. George Honey also had an engage-
ment. The pantomime this Christmas was called *Birds*,

Beasts, and Fishes. Another posthumous play by Wilkins, with the melodramatic title, *Money and Misery*, ran for several weeks early in 1855. Searle and Rayner were the leading actors at this time. Mr. Charles Pitt, "the established tragedian," played in *The Robbers* of Schiller, at the end of May, and on Monday, the 11th of June, Mr. Charles Matthews, with several members of the lately disbanded Lyceum company, migrated to the far East, and met with a real success. Their engagement lasted for four weeks. Mr. N. T. Hicks took the lead again, during Mr. Searle's tenancy in July and August. Mr. Pitt returned for the beginning of the winter season, and was followed by an English opera company, consisting of Misses Rebecca Issacs and Dyer, Mr. Leffler, Mr. George Tedder, and Mr. Augustus Braham, under the conductorship of Mr. F. Kingsbury. The operas were quite a hit, and were continued up to Christmas, when *The Fox and the Grapes* served to introduce a new and exceedingly clever clown, Mr. Forrest. This pantomime ran till Easter in the following year.

The following is a specimen of the grandiloquent tone which pervaded the announcements of the City of London Theatre about this time. " None," to quote the *affiches*, " but managers who really study their profession, can tell the anxiety in catering for the public, how delightful it is when their labour, and untiring zeal, is rewarded by a success like the one attending the new drama." This imposing, but rather illiterate, prelude had reference to a spectral play, *Selfishness*, brought out in February, 1856, and which was very well acted by N. T. Hicks, W. Travers,

F 2

W. Searle, and Miss Marian Lacy. "Its originality," said the bills, "was beyond conception." Nevertheless, "the monster drama" only ran three weeks !

Mdlle. Nau, once a *prima donna* of high repute in Paris, and who might be remembered as singing for Mr. Maddox at the Princess's Theatre, some time before, headed an English opera company at Easter. Another drama by Wilkins, *The Frost of Youth*, inaugurated the winter season, and was followed by a very interesting experiment, namely, the reintroduction, at a long interval, of Mr. and Miss Vandenhoff, to an eastern public. These performers, who belonged essentially to the Kemble school of acting, had not for many years condescended to the star system of such houses as the City of London, and their appearance on Monday, the 27th of October, in Lovell's beautiful and touching play, *Love's Sacrifice*, excited no little interest in histrionic circles. Their success was complete. The great situation, at the end of the fourth act, was elaborately worked up by both, and the curtain fell to literally unbounded applause. *Love's Sacrifice* was followed by Talfourd's *Ion, Romeo and Juliet*, and by Miss Vandenhoff's own play,⁵ *Woman's Heart*, in all of which they maintained, and, indeed, strengthened, the impression first made, and their engagement forms another feature in the history of this theatre. The pantomime, *Anne Boleyn*, was the two hundredth con- cocted by Mr. Nelson Lee. Mr. Forrest was again the

---

⁵ Originally produced at the Haymarket Theatre, on Saturday, the 14th of February, 1852.

Clown. It ran nearly till Easter, 1857, when Mr. Charles Pitt returned to play in a new drama, *The Spanish Girl.* The summer season was conducted, as usual, by Mr. William Searle. At the commencement of the winter the African Roscius, Mr. Ira Aldridge, was playing *Othello,* Zanga in the tragedy of *The Revenge,* and Gambia in the pretty old musical drama of *The Slave.* Messrs. Johnson, and Nelson Lee, had some months previously offered a premium for the best specimen of "domestic" drama sent in. This resulted in the production of *Lucy Wentworth, or the Village-born Beauty,* by a Mr. Priest, given at the end of October. The plot was of the simplest character, but the principal situations had considerable pathos, and altogether it proved quite successful. The only other instances of prize dramas which occur to us are Mr. Webster's 500*l.* premium, for the best specimen of comedy at the Haymarket, which resulted in the acceptance, and failure, of Mrs. Gore's *Quid pro Quo,* in 1844; and the T. P. Cooke prize nautical drama of *True to the Core,* by Mr. A. R. Selous, in 1866, at the Surrey. The pantomime of *William the Second,* with the "inimitable and unapproachable" clown, Mr. Forrest, was a hit.

A play of the "Susan Hopley" species, entitled *A Poor Girl's Temptations,* by Mr. W. Travers, in which the heroine was impersonated by Miss Augusta Clifton, proved attractive, in March, 1858, and at Easter, the Australian actors, Mr. and Mrs. Clarence Holt, formerly lessees of the Marylebone Theatre, appeared in a new drama, *The Secret Passion.* Mr. Searle's summer season commenced on the 31st of May. The theatre was very handsomely re-decorated during the autumn, and re-opened on Monday, the 20th of September, with a new domestic drama, of "strong interest," entitled *Twenty Years in a Debtors' Prison*, from the apparently inexhaustible pen of Mr. Wilkins, supported by Messrs. W. Searle, W. Travers, Beaumont Hughes, E. Shirra, Misses Augusta Clifton, Laporte, and Mrs. Moreton Brookes, a very good working *corps*. This was succeeded by another, *The Woman of the World*, adapted by Mr. Nelson Lee, from a story in Reynolds' Miscellany. According to the bills, this achieved "a paramount success, never before excelled." Mr. T. C. King was to have appeared in November, but was obliged, through illness, to cancel his engagement. The pantomime, *King Comet and Prince Quicksilver*, was as successful as usual, but the new clown, a Mr. Harvey Teesdale, made only a moderate impression. Solomon's very dramatic picture, *Waiting for the Verdict*, suggested a drama, upon the same subject, to a Mr. Hazlewood, which was successfully produced in January, 1859, and ran for thirty or forty nights. Mr. Edmund Falconer's excellent comedy, *The Extremes*, was mounted at Easter, with Mr. John Neville and Mrs. Weston in the leading parts. A drama, *Woman's Wrongs*, by Mr. Courtney, was the first event of the winter season, but, generally speaking, the performances, up to Christmas, presented no feature of interest. The pantomime was a parody of Home's tragedy, *Douglas*, under the title of *Young Norval on the Grampian Hills*, and introduced one, whom it was indeed no empty puff to describe as "the great little

Huline," the favourite clown from the Princess's Theatre. The clown and the pantomime were each a hit.

The old spectacle of *The Prophet* was revived at Easter, 1860, and was followed by a burlesque on *Jane Shore*, which proved a failure. Mr. T. C. King made his *début* on Monday, the 30th of April, in *Hamlet*, and during his engagement played also such parts as Claude Melnotte, Othello, and Macbeth. Mr. Nelson Lee's repeated attempts to popularize the highest class of the drama were in the highest degree creditable to him, but his system of puffery was only worthy of Richardson [6]—to whose booth and business, by the bye, he had in former days succeeded. Such paragraphs, moreover, as "the king's name is a tower of strength," at the head of the playbills, were quite inadmissible. On the termination of Mr. T. C. King's engagement, the theatre again reverted to Mr. William Searle. Mr. Harry Widdicombe, and Miss Charlotte Saunders, appeared for the benefit of Mrs. John Wilkins, on Tuesday, the 7th of August, and Mr. N. T. Hicks was again here for a short time in September. The winter season began at Michaelmas with melodrama: *The Thieves' Secret, The Criminal's Flight, The Guilty Mother*, and *Chaunting Ben of Spitalfields*, were specimens of the fare now set before the public. Better things came with the return, early in December, of Mr. T. C.

[6] A celebrated travelling showman, who flourished during the earlier portion of the present century. Richardson's itinerant theatre, in fact, formed the professional cradle of more than one actor, who subsequently achieved metropolitan distinction.

King, whose acting in *Othello*, *Hamlet*, and *Virginius* was much admired for its power and finish. Miss Edith Heraud played for Mr. King's benefit on Tuesday, the 18th of December. The pantomime was *Fair Rosamond*, with a new and good clown, Lupino.

A new play of some merit, *The Star of the Woodlands*, by Mr. Nelson Lee, Jun., was successfully brought out in March, 1861. *Waiting for the Verdict* was revived at Easter, for the introduction of Mr. Graham, the favourite actor from the Princess's, and was followed by *The Green Hills of the Far West*, the best and most popular of all the earlier pieces written by Mr. Wilkins. Mr. Graham was also appointed to the post of stage-manager. The old melodrama of *The Miller and His Men* was given, with all the original music, at the end of April. Mr. Nelson Lee continued to direct the summer season, and early in June Mdme. Celeste accepted an engagement, and came out in *The House on the Bridge of Notre-Dame*. Mr. Charles Mortimer, Mr. Morelli, and Mr. Gomersal were members of the company at this time. Mr. Charles Verner was engaged for lead, and stage-management, at the beginning of the winter, and played in *Richelieu*, for Mr. Johnson's benefit, on Tuesday, the 10th of December. The pantomime was *Alonzo the Brave*, with Lupino as clown. *The Idiot of the Mountain*, a version of a popular Surrey drama, was the first novelty of the year 1862. Mr. Lee's pantomime ran up to the 22nd of March. Mr. Travers attempted a summer season on Whit Monday, the 9th of June. The theatre reopened for the winter, rather later than usual, on Monday, the 20th of October, with Mr. Gustavus Brooke, as Sir Giles Overreach, in *A New Way to pay Old Debts*. Mr. Brooke played Brutus in *Julius Cæsar*, supported by Mr. Ryder as Cassius, and Mr. J. F. Young, a rising actor, as Mark Antony, on Monday, the 24th of November. The *First Part of King Henry the Fourth* was given on Monday, the 8th of December, with Mr. Brooke as Hotspur, Mr. Young as Prince Henry, and Mr. Ryder as Sir John Falstaff. Mr. Brooke concluded an engagement, equally creditable to himself, and the theatre, with a performance of Sheridan Knowles' *William Tell*, on Monday, the 22nd of the same month, and on Boxing-night Miss Harriet Coveney appeared in the pantomime, *Sing a Song of Sixpence*. A new clown from the provinces, Mr. William Mathews, proved a particularly neat jumper.

The "laurel-crowned" pantomime ran till the 1st of March, 1863, when Mr. James Anderson played for a month, in *The Robbers*, *Ingomar*, and *Civilization*. Mr. Young opened at Whitsuntide with a new drama, *Bow Bells*. An English opera company, consisting of Miss Anna Hiles, Mdme. Laura Baxter, Mr. Patey, Mr. Aynsley Cook, Mr. St. Albyn, and Mr. George Perren, sang in July. On Saturday, the 3rd of October, the City reopened for the winter, under the sole lesseeship of Mr. Nelson Lee, with Falconer's *Peep O'Day*, prefaced by an inaugural address, from the practised and skilful pen of Mr. E. L. Blanchard, and spoken by Mr. J. F. Young, the stage-manager, which we transcribe :—

"Ladies and Gentlemen,—I'm not quite sure,
But rather think you've heard those words before.

Well, true it is, and, pity 'tis, 'tis true,
It isn't easy now to say what's new ;
Unless, indeed, some novelty was found
In lines that run a long way under-ground,
Or, 'twixt yourselves, me, and the *Morning Post,*
Raising our fashionable friend, The Ghost.
But, you all know, this house attention merits,
As being the proper place to raise *your* spirits,
To stir your hearts with dramas quite domestic,
Or raise a jest, maybe, in style majestic ;
In fact, a Public House and sign to borrow,
A House of Call, and call again to-morrow.
But stop, for my appearance there must be
Some sort of motive—dear me, let me see—
I know.   On this which is our opening day,
Something particular I had to say ;
But in my haste to see your welcome faces
I've lost my part and can't tell where the place is.
There's one line in the play-bill, I am sure—
   ' Places secured each day from ten to four.'
Well, now to frankly put the present case,
I, as a servant here, must know my place ;
And having got it, I come forth to say,
This really is a most important day.
' If why ? ' you ask, I answer, ' For this reason,'
It is the opening of our Winter season.
When your old favourite, Worthy Nelson Lee,
Becomes, as well becomes *him,* Sole Lessee ;
Though Sole Lessee he's only from this minute,
You all well know his soul has long been in it.
To brevity the soul of wit being debtor,
The Lessee thinks the less he says the better ;
Yet though he says but little, he will do
A great deal, if he's patronized by you.
Leaving his acts to show, as each month passes,
His three-act dramas and his one-act farces ;

And as his modesty cuts short his speech,
For him your vote and interest, I beseech.
You know how long he has woven Christmas rhymes,
Making you laugh with roaring pantomimes,
How many hundreds he has penn'd, remember,
That flung a sunbeam into dark December.
Well, now he asks you to assist in one
Of the best openings he has ever done,
Seeking your aid to kindly help him o'er
A change of scene he never had before.
You know his industry—that *never* fails,
Just raise a breeze, enough to fill his sails ;
And this stout craft, all sands and shoals safe past,
With him for Pilot, will reach home at last.
Our freighted ship thus starts on Fortune's ocean,
Where Lee is now, I've not the slightest notion ;
But when there's any risk, my cry will be,
Brisk, boys ; look out a-head, and Helm-a-Lee !
In days of old, for England, home, and beauty,
Nelson expected all to do their duty ;
And in the present day we've nought to fear,
Our Nelson's motto always is ' I am here ! '
And being here to give all satisfaction,
So pipe all hands and clear the deck for action."

Mr. George Belmore appeared in *The Deal Boatman*
at the end of October, and Mr. Ryder returned for three
nights, the 21st, 22nd, and 23rd of December. *Harlequin
Blackbeard ; or, Old Dame Trot and her Comical Cat*,
was the pantomime, with Mr. William Mathews as clown,
and Mr. Morelli, an excellent pantaloon.

Caught at Last was the title of a new drama, written
by the lessee, and produced at Easter, 1864. On Tuesday, the 3rd of April, Mr. Benjamin Webster appeared in
One Touch of Nature, and Paul Bedford—glorious Paul

—sang a comic song for the benefit of Mr. Nelson Lee. A Mr. Frederick Marchant was manager for the summer. Byron's *Manfred* was given, with appropriate scenic effects, on the 25th of June, Mr. Alfred Rayner playing the *title rôle*. The house again opened for the winter on Monday, the 10th of October. Mr. and Mrs. Clarence Holt played in the legitimate drama for four or five weeks in November and December, and on the 26th of the latter month, *The King of the Golden Valley* was produced, with "a clown and a half" in the persons of Mr. Huline and his youthful son. This pantomime ran up to the 11th of March, 1865. An imitator of the celebrated equestrian, Adah Isaacs Menken, who styled herself "the beautiful Menkon," performed in *Mazeppa* in April, but failed to make an impression. Mr. Nelson Lee, although still retaining the lesseeship, had now retired from all active share in the management, which devolved upon Messrs. Marchant and Travers. Mr. Creswick had an engagement in July, and appeared in the *Flower Girl*, *Virginius*, and *Othello*. Mr. Alfred Rayner played Cardinal Wolsey in September, and Miss Jane Coveney joined the company in October. *Othello* was mounted with some care in November, to introduce a Mr. Newton Gotthold as the Moor, Mr. William Travers as Iago, Miss Le Thière as Emilia, and Miss Ada Cavendish, Desdemona. The pantomime, *King Flame*, was written by Nelson Lee. Some of the survivors of the ill-fated ship, "London," were induced to exhibit themselves on the stage, for a few weeks, in February, 1866. The house was opened in July by Mr. Waldron, a good actor, with a version of the

Porte St. Martin drama, *Le Bossu*, but the new management came to an abrupt termination during the autumn,
and Mr. Douglas, who had just been burnt out of the
neighbouring Standard Theatre, transferred his company
to the City of London at the beginning of November.
Mr. Nelson Lee again furnished the pantomime, entitled,
Ding, Dong, Dell. A very young girl who figured in it as
Miss Constance, has since become better known as Miss
Constance Loseby, the popular burlesque actress and
singer. The clowns were Almonti and Delevanti.

Miss Sarah Thorne played in January, 1867. Burton's
Christy Minstrels occupied the house in Lent. At Easter
it reopened under Mr. Morris Abrahams, of the Effingham Theatre, with a very good company, comprising Mr.
T. Mead, Mr. David Jones, Mr. Brittain Wright, Mr.
William Spencer, and Miss Fanny Bennet. The performances—one constant round of very inferior melodramas—call for no sort of observation, except that the
excellent actor Mr. T. Mead seceded from the theatre at
the end of November. Mr. Nelson Lee contributed the
Christmas novelty once more. Its title was *Wat Tyler ;
or, Love, War, and Peace.* The pantomime—owing to
the rival attractions of the new Standard Theatre, lately
rebuilt on a greatly extended scale—came to an untimely
end about the middle of January, 1868, and the house reopened as a circus under the direction of Herr Dassie.
On the 1st of March Mr. Nelson Lee announced the
theatre to let, but his advertisement of " great chance for
a start in management," seemed to offer small inducement to any one, since no candidate appeared to be

forthcoming. Captain Horton Rhys, however, ventured at Easter to produce a drama, *Ellie Brandon; or, Revenge and Love*, in which Miss Catherine Lucette, Miss Julia Seaman, Mr. Lewis Ball, Mr. Dolman, Mr. Dudley, and the author played. The management and company were of a higher class than those immediately preceding them, but the house had sunk to so low an ebb—the people in the boxes smoking their short pipes during the perform-ance—that the speculation was abandoned within a fort-night, and the City was again advertised to let, " on most moderate terms."

Mr. George Webster—brother of the proprietor of the Adelphi—next tried his hand, with a melodrama by J. B. Johnstone, *Paved with Gold*, and a *ballet-divertissement*, in which the *cancan* was announced to be danced by " a bevy of the most lovely and graceful ballet ladies in the world." This *ballet* was in itself a sufficient indication of the sort of management to be attempted there. It lasted, however, only for a *week*. At the end of June the luckless little house was again opened, under the quadruple guidance of Messrs. Harmer, Wright, Lane, and Roberts, with a drama, *Our dear old Home*, in which the hideous spec-tacle of a corpse, laid out in a winding-sheet, with the moonlight playing upon its features, was introduced as the sensation of the piece ! The theatre soon closed again, and in August Mr. Nelson Lee sold the property to the Great Eastern Railway Company for 6000*l.*, who relet it to a Mr. Harrison for music-hall purposes. The place was then reopened, at prices varying from 3*d.* to 1*d.* In other words, the City of London Theatre, which, for thirty years had held its own so bravely amongst the Minors, and upon the boards of which so many of our leading actors and actresses had not disdained to tread, had at last descended to the level of a Penny Gaff!! It is unnecessary to pursue the story further. Enough that —happily for the neighbourhood—this last and worst state of things has ceased to be; that the building has long since been converted to other uses. The exterior, indeed, is still the same. The classic front remains unchanged, to mark the spot, and " point a moral " to the passer-by. But its old frequenters know it no more, for the graceful columns now merely serve to shelter and support—a *Soup-Kitchen.*

At the present date—April, 1883—the City of London Theatre has undergone another change. The portion formerly occupied by the stage has been absorbed by the Great Eastern Railway; but the auditorium and entrances, which retain all their former features, have been leased to the East Central Temperance Association, who now utilize the place for Sunday, and occasional week-day, services, the other nights being set apart for cheap concerts, on a similar scale to those adopted with such good results at the Victoria Coffee Palace and Music Hall. In its latest capacity the building is recognized as a boon to the surrounding district.

THE DRAMA IN PORTMAN-MARKET.

Another MINOR RECORD.

THE Marylebone Theatre? Where is it? Such, probably, would be the response of any, save the most in-
veterate, or veteran playgoer, when interrogated as to his
knowledge of the edifice in question. Yet though this
modest temple of the muses—located, as its name implies,
in the north-western district of the metropolis—has, for
several years, relapsed into the obscurity which charac-
terized its earlier existence, the Marylebone Theatre
possesses, nevertheless, a history of its own, and, in days
long past, could boast of more than one management,
whose intelligent efforts to popularize the best specimens
of the Poetic Drama were fully recognized, and fairly
supported, by the general public.

The Marylebone Theatre, then, is situated in Church
Street, a thoroughfare which connects Portman-Market
with the northern extremity of Edgware Road. It
occupies, with considerable additions, the site of a much
smaller house, known as the Pavilion Theatre, and which
existed as early as 1832. The Pavilion being unlicensed,
tickets of admission were sold, at a baker's shop, opposite

the theatre, and at the old Salisbury coffee-house. The prices of admission at this time, were—Boxes, two shillings; Pit, one shilling; Gallery, sixpence. Mr. Henry Widdicomb, and Mr. Cony, who later became famous, respectively, as low comedian, and pantomimist, were at first the leading players, and, although the performances were, generally speaking, of the humblest description, we have met with an old bill in which *The Rivals*, of Sheridan, was announced for the evening of the 28th of May, in this year. A comic song by Widdicomb seemed to be the invariable accompaniment of every play-bill. On Whit Monday, the 11th of June, young Grimaldi began a two-weeks' engagement, during which he appeared, as Man Friday, in *Robinson Crusoe*, as Black Cæsar in *The Fatal Thicket*, and as Scaramouch in *Don Juan*. On Friday, the 22nd of June, he played clown, in a scene from *Mother Goose*, and gave his father's famous song, "Hot Codlings." Mr. William West was playing Dr. Ollapod, in *The Poor Gentleman*, during the following week, and the clown, Paulo, lent his services for Mr. Wallbourn's benefit, on Thursday, the 5th of July. Mr. Edward Wright, in years to come, the favourite comic actor of the Adelphi, was in the company, in November. The name of Mr. Edward Edwards appears as playing here, in 1833. He was better known later, as Mr. Edward Giovanelli. The universally popular comedian, Vale, played Dick Drudge, in Douglas Jerrold's drama, *Nell Gwynne*, on the 8th of March, in this year. On Friday, the 21st of March, 1834, the song "Serjeant Slum" was sung, between the parts of the performance, by Master Joseph Cave, "his first appearance on any stage."

This boy will be readily recognized, as the present proprietor of the Marylebone. In 1835, the name of the house
was changed to that of the Portman Theatre. Rather later
on it was rebuilt by a Mr. Leveridge, and opened, with
the new title of the Marylebone Theatre, under the
management of Mr. Hyde, on Monday, the 13th of November, 1837. That the new theatre was still to appeal
exclusively to the humbler inhabitants of its, even then,
thickly populated neighbourhood, might be inferred from
the nature of the first night's programme, which offered
nothing better than a melodrama, entitled *The Beggar's
Haunt, or Fortune's Changes.* The only names of any
mark, in the new company, were those of Cobham—
looked upon, in his time, as the Kemble of the minor
theatres—and Mr. J. W. Ray, who developed, later, into
a comedian of more than average ability. There was a
pantomime at Christmas, preceded by Lillo's old tragedy,
George Barnwell, and early in the ensuing year we find
such plays as *Pizarro, Jane Shore*, and *John Bull* in the
bills, but the venture apparently did not prosper, and
the house eventually closed for some months. It was
reopened for the winter season of 1838-9, by Mr. Johnson and Mr. Nelson Lee, with a company which included
the names of Attwood, John Douglass, Fenton, Collins,
the pantomimist, Paul Herring, Miss Thornton, and
Mrs. Stanley. As the results, however, did not appear to
be favourable, they abandoned it, early in the summer, to
Mr. Fox Cooper, who did not long continue his speculation.

We have failed to discover any trace of its doings in
the two following years, during which the place probably

remained shut up altogether, but it seems to have been, in a great measure, reconstructed in 1842, and was reopened on Monday, the 12th of December, in that year, as the New Theatre-Royal, Marylebone, under the lesseeship of Mr. Douglass, and the stage-management of Mr. Edward Stirling—always a reliable name. The new theatre was built to accommodate 2300 people, and was pronounced very handsome. The list of performers comprised the names of Freer, Attwood, Rayner, and Cobham. Mr. Osbaldiston and Miss Vincent played during the following week, and Mr. Nelson Lee provided a new panto-mime at Christmas.

The house, at length fairly started, remained, for some years, in the hands of Mr. Douglass, whose management not only answered, in a pecuniary sense, but was charac-terized by a good deal of spirit and energy. Its more noticeable events were as follows : Mrs. Waylett, a de-lightful singer, and actress, in her day, appeared in February, 1843, and Freer also played in *Rob Roy*, as well as in the now forgotten, but once famous melo-drama, *One o'Clock, or the Knight and the Wood-Demon ;* another fossil, the burlesque of *Bombastes Furioso*, was in the bills, a few months later ; and in December, the *Coriolanus* of Shakspeare was respectably represented. Freer, Charles Dillon, the tragedian, Mr. Otway, and Mrs. W. West, were the leading players throughout this year, as well as during the greater part of the year 1844. In March of the latter, *The Castle Spectre* of Monk Lewis was given, with success. On its original production, at Drury Lane, in 1797, Kemble and Sarah Siddons had not felt themselves above appearing in this play, which was long the favourite ghost drama of every theatre, or even barn, throughout the United Kingdom. That it has now to a great extent become obsolete, is probably due to an improved taste, which declines to tolerate the inflated language which Mat Lewis has put into the mouths of his leading characters. Yet, to a purely melo-dramatic audience, *The Castle Spectre* must ever prove attractive, owing to the cleverness of the various situa-tions, and the admirable skill with which the interest is led up to the several appearances of the ghost. Although its kind may not be of the best, the old play is still the best of its kind ; and, as a matter of fact, under the slightly altered title of *The Spectre of Conway Castle*, it remains to this day a stock piece in the repertory of the theatre in Portman-Market.

Wright, Paul Bedford, and Miss Emma Stanley were engaged in September, 1844, and were followed by Mr. Denvil, in Lord Byron's *Manfred.* A Mr. Hudson Kirby played on Wednesday, December 17th, for the benefit of that once popular transpontine manager, Mr. Almar. For Mr. Douglass's benefit, early in 1845, Wright and Paul Bedford again acted, in company with Widdicombe, Cony, Blanchard, and Mr. E. F. Saville. When the theatre reopened for the winter of this year, the celebrated *mime*, Wieland, was engaged to play the *Imp* in the ballet-pantomime, *The Daughter of the Danube.* In October, Mr. and Mrs. Honner were to be seen in the pretty old drama, *Mary, the Maid of the Inn.* A Mr. Grattan Dawson also " starred," in *Macbeth* and other plays. The clown, Paul Herring, was engaged for Easter, 1846. Mr. Rayner appeared as Hamlet, in January, 1847, and afterwards, the American Dwarf, Tom Thumb, was exhibited. In February, Mr. Bayntun Rolt played in *King Richard III.*, and a transatlantic actor, Mr. J. R. Scott, in *Pizarro*, and *Damon and Pythias*. Mr. Charles Dillon returned at Easter, in *Don Cæsar de Bazan*. These efforts at legitimacy, though not without merit, were all of the rough-and-ready order, and were alternated, it may be added, with such sorry doings as *Paul the Poacher, Jack Ketch, Bone Squash, The Last Link of Love, Sarah the Jewess, or the Extorted Oath*, and lastly by a piece with the sonorous title, *The Royal Crusader, or the Black Brand of Rome !*

Mr. Douglass's management terminated at the end of June, 1847, and on the 1st of the following August, an announcement appeared in the daily papers that Mrs. Warner, who had recently withdrawn from Sadler's Wells —then, and long afterwards, under the ever-memorable direction of Phelps and Greenwood,—had taken the Marylebone Theatre. Mrs. Warner, in her preliminary circular, promised "the performance of such plays as may appear best suited to the resources of the establishment," and added that "an earnest endeavour will be made to illustrate these plays appropriately and effectively. The engagement of a company, selected with a reference to the task of duly rendering the text of the great dramatic authors, the assistance of artists of the first competence, in the scenic and mechanical departments, and the liberal and careful provision of all the other accessories

to the histrionic art, will, it is hoped, enable the management to accomplish this purpose."

Having been thoroughly cleansed and re-decorated,
the house opened for the season, on Monday, the 30th
of August, with Shakspeare's play, *A Winter's Tale,* in
which it is needless to say that Mrs. Warner played
Hermione—one of her finest parts—in her finest manner,
and was well supported by Mrs. Tyrrell, as Paulina, by
Miss Angell, a pleasing young actress, from Bath, as
Perdita, and by another and very clever *débutante*, from
Birmingham, Miss Charlotte Saunders, as Mopsa. Mr.
Graham, a prominent member, some years previously,
of Macready's company at Drury Lane, was the Leontes
of the night, Mr. James Johnstone, from Liverpool,
Polixenes ; Mr. George Vining, also from Bath, Florizel ;
and an excellent Autolycus was discovered, in Mr. Henry
Webb, who though almost unknown to London, had long
enjoyed exceptional popularity, as a comedian, throughout the provinces. Generally speaking, the performance
was of the most careful kind. The scenery and accessories, as promised beforehand, were rich, and in good
taste, and the whole entertainment augured well for the
success of the experiment.

A Winter's Tale was followed by *The Hunchback* and
The School for Scandal, both of which were acted and
mounted with equal propriety, and on Monday, the 11th
of October, *Hamlet* was produced in a very artistic
manner. Mrs. Warner, herself, did not disdain the part
of Gertrude, and Ophelia was judiciously performed by
Miss Huddart. The Hamlet of Mr. Graham had many

good points, and Mr. James Johnstone exhibited no mean elocutionary power as Claudius. Mr. Belton was the Laertes, Mr. Harvey, Polonius. Mr. Henry Webb developed a rich fund of humour as the First Gravedigger, and all the subordinate parts were well-filled. The *mise-en-scène* was of the most creditable description, and, in particular, the comings and goings of the Ghost were so ingeniously contrived as to make this revival, for the time being, quite the talk of the town. The Ghost itself, by the way, found an efficient, though rather youthful representative, in the person of Mr. George Vining. *The Gamester*, *The Jealous Wife*, and *The Provoked Husband*, with Mrs. Warner as Mrs. Beverley, Mrs. Oakley, and Lady Townly, respectively, were next given, in addition to *The Bridal*,—as Sheridan Knowles's not very felicitous alteration of Beaumont and Fletcher's pathetic *Maid's Tragedy* was called—with Mr. George Vining as Melantius, Miss Angell, Aspatia, and the Manageress, Evadne —a part which she might be truly said to have made her own.

On Monday, the 29th of November, an almost unique experiment was made in the revival of Beaumont and Fletcher's comedy, *The Scornful Lady*, skilfully purified, and adapted to the modern stage, by Mr. T. J. Serle. *The Scornful Lady* had not been seen in London since March, 1746, when it was given at Drury Lane, for Mrs. Woffington's benefit—if we except a version under the title of *The Capricious Lady*, produced, for the celebrated Mrs. Abington, at Covent Garden, in 1783. The heroine of this comedy is a lady—anonymous—who from pride, conceals in public, the love which she really cherishes for her admirer, the Elder Loveless. Loveless having kissed her in the presence of company, the lady banishes him, for a year's travel in France. Apparently complying, he departs, leaving his house, and estate, to the care of a spendthrift brother, the Younger Loveless, who is under the surveillance, however, of his steward, Savil. The steward proves unfaithful to his trust, and mingles with the younger brother and his boon companions—a Captain, a Traveller, a Poet, and a Tobacco-man—in every description of wild revelry. Meanwhile, the elder brother returns, disguised as a mariner, and introduces himself as a friend of the exiled lover, whom he describes as having been drowned at sea. This intelligence induces an usurer, Morecraft, to offer a sum of 6000*l* to the prodigal, as the price of his brother's estate. The lady, meanwhile, has detected her lover's disguise, and retorts on his stratagem by feigning a willingness to console herself with the attentions of another suitor, Wilford. The Elder Loveless then declares himself, and the lady repeats her sentence of banishment. He retaliates by laughing at her, and the lady swoons. Worked upon by this, Loveless is unable to maintain his show of indifference. Whereupon the lady recovers, and overwhelms him with ridicule. He forthwith affects to abandon his suit altogether, and goes so far as to introduce Wilford, in the disguise of a woman, as the mistress whom he intends to marry. This last device brings the scornful lady to terms. She consents to an immediate union, and Wilford is compensated with the hand of her sister, Martha. There is also an amusing

underplot—very coarse, in the original version—bearing
upon the courtship of the Lady's curate, Sir Roger, and
her waiting-gentlewoman, Abigail. The cast of *The
Scornful Lady* at the Marylebone was as follows :—

Elder Loveless	Mr. Graham.
Younger Loveless	Mr. Belton.
Welford	Mr. George Vining.
Morecraft	Mr. Harvey.
Savil	Mr. George Cooke.
Sir Roger	Mr. Henry Webb.
Captain	Mr. James Johnstone.
Traveller	Mr. Potter.
Poet	Mr. Saunders.
Tobacco-man	Mr. Rolfe.
Abigail	Miss Charlotte Saunders.
Martha	Miss Huddart.
The Lady	Mrs. Warner.

Every one of these characters was thoroughly well
played, and the Scornful Lady of Mrs. Warner stood out
as a histrionic portrait, which will long remain a tradition
in the annals of the modern stage.

The manner in which this fine comedy was mounted,
reflected, no less than its presentment, the highest credit
on the management. The scenery, dresses, and decorations, were remarkable for their correctness, in a day when
research, and accuracy, were so far less sought after, than
is the case at the present time. The interiors, in which
the action was laid, were all compiled from historical
sources, and one truly magnificent scene, the Lady's
Parlour, with its chimney-piece of white Carrara marble,
china vases, and clocks, and the *then* luxury—at 1616,

the date of the play—of small carpets, was simply a marvel of completeness and refined taste. The grand old play proved worthy of its mounting, and was unanimously received, by a house filled to overflowing with artists, critics, and *litterati*, with every token of the most unqualified success.

The Scornful Lady ran up to Christmas, when an excellent pantomime, by Mr. E. L. Blanchard, entitled *Eyes, Nose, and Mouth*, was brought out, with Tom Matthews, the acknowledged legitimate successor of Grimaldi, as clown. *The Lady of Lyons*, in which Mr. George Vining performed Claude Melnotte, was given in January, 1848, and on the last day of that month, Massinger's *A New Way to Pay Old Debts* was put up. Here, Mr. Graham, as Sir Giles Overreach, had to measure weapons with Mr. Gustavus Brooke, who, then in the first flush of his metropolitan fame, was playing the same character at the Olympic—and was not worsted in the encounter.

The Wrecker's Daughter, by Sheridan Knowles, with Mrs. Warner in her original part of Marian, was the next revival, and, subsequently, Shiel's *Damon and Pythias*, Sothern's *Isabella, or the Fatal Marriage*, and Lovell's beautiful play, *Love's Sacrifice*—with Miss Fanny Vining as Margaret Aylmer—were given, as well as a new fairy extravaganza, *The Enchanted Tower*, by Mr. Charles Selby, in which the more juvenile. members of the company were exhibited to advantage.

Mrs. Warner now made another raid upon the Elizabethan Drama, and produced on Monday, the 2nd of April, Beaumont and Fletcher's tragedy, or, rather tragic

melodrama, *The Double Marriage*, with the subjoined
cast :—

Juliana	. . . . .	Mrs. Warner.
Martia	. . . . .	Miss Fanny Vining.
Lucio	. . . . .	Miss Charlotte Saunders.
Ferrand	. . . . .	Mr. Lacy.
Virolet	. . . . .	Mr. Graham.
Brissonet	. . . .	Mr. James Johnstone.
Camillo	. . . . .	Mr. Tindall.
Rouvere	. . . . .	Mr. Potter.
Villio	. . . . .	Mr. Henry Webb.
Castruccio	. . . .	Mr. George Vining.
Pandulpho	. . . .	Mr. Clifford.
Duke of Sesse	. . .	Mr. Johnstone.
Ascanio	. . . . .	Mr. Belton.
Boatswain	. . . .	Mr. George Cooke.
Master	. . . . .	Mr. Howell.
Gunner	. . . . .	Mr. Saunders.

The story is as follows :—

Virolet, a Neapolitan noble, plots with some friends to
effect the downfall of Ferrand, King of Naples, but is
betrayed by Rouvere, and concealed by his wife Juliana,
who, in consequence, is put to the torture. He is then
liberated, and sent on a maritime expedition. This brings
the first act to a conclusion. In the second, Virolet is
captured by a proscribed Duke of Sesse—now turned
pirate—brought on board his ship, and drawn into con-
tracting a second marriage—unknown to her father—with
the Duke's daughter, Martia. He escapes with his new
wife in one of the ship's boats, and is forthwith pursued
by the pirates. The third act finds them all assembled

at Naples; depicts the various phases of court life, and the humours of a royal favourite, Castruccio, who has been given permission to assume, for one day, the robes and authority of the King.   Next occurs a stormy meeting between Juliana, Martia, and Virolet.   A divorce is arranged between Virolet and his first wife, but the second is simultaneously informed, that her marriage must remain merely nominal.   Meanwhile, the Duke, and his band, conspire to revenge themselves on Ferrand, Virolet, and Martia at once.   At the beginning of the fourth act, we find the pirates enrolled as guards in the service of the King.   Martia visits Juliana for the purpose of insulting her, and threatens to be revenged upon Virolet, for her disappointment.   Juliana seeks Virolet, to warn him of his danger.   Their interview is broken in upon by Martia, who disdainfully gives him back " his love, his vow," and then proceeds, with Rouvere, to sell her honour to the King, as the price of his assistance, in her scheme of vengeance.   The Duke and Virolet, in the meantime, have formed a counter-plot against Ferrand, and the latter assumes the dress of Rouvere in order to obtain access more easily to his sovereign, whom he intends to slay. But Juliana had also conceived the purpose of assassinating Rouvere, and, encountering her husband, wounds him mortally, by mistake.   The popular commotion, set on foot by the pirates, now grows higher, and in the midst of it the King himself is killed by Sesse.   Then lastly comes the terrible interview between the Duke and his infamous daughter, which is ended by the Boatswain stabbing the latter, and excusing the act thus :—

"I confess
That she deserved to die ; but by whose hand ?
Not by a father's. Double all her guilt,
It could not make you innocent, had you done it ;
In *me* 'tis murder ; in *you* 'twere a crime
Heaven could not pardon. Witness that I love you !
And in that love I did it."

This formed a striking and unlooked-for *dénoûment*, which brought the piece to a triumphant conclusion.

This play, rearranged with much ability by Mr. Serle, cannot be considered as amongst the author's best. As may be inferred from the above description, its plot has no lack of incident. But the incidents are over-crowded, and for the most part revolting, whilst the characters, from the weak-minded, vacillating, Virolet, to the worthless Martia, are one and all repulsive, if we except the devoted, and deeply-wronged, Juliana, portrayed, on this occasion—specially in the torture-scene—with powerful, and admirably sustained, skill by Mrs. Warner, who had been rarely seen to greater advantage. *The Double Marriage*, nevertheless, abounds in effective situations—Beaumont and Fletcher were complete masters of stage-effect—more particularly the scenes between Juliana, Virolet, and Martia, which were followed with unmistakable interest by the audience. As a whole, however, the impression which it made was not equal to that of *The Scornful Lady*, though, as a theatrical curiosity—it had not been given in London since 1683—it was interesting to amateurs, and did not detract from, if it did not add to, the high reputation won by Mrs. Warner for her management. The drama was superbly mounted, and the scenery of Mr. Cuthbert, which included the deck of the ship—a very elaborate set—the Pirate Chief's cabin, an antique chamber in the palace, and a view of Naples, seen through a ruined archway, was universally admired.

The Double Marriage tided the theatre on till Easter, when Macready came over for a short series of performances, in *Hamlet*, *Othello*, and *Macbeth*. In these plays, he was supported by the Ghost, Iago, and Macduff, of Mr. Henry Marston. Mrs. Warner, as before, played Gertrude, nor did she consider Emilia beneath her talents. Her Lady Macbeth had long been held, by old playgoers, as by far the finest seen, since the days of the famous Mrs. Siddons. With a revival of *King Henry VIII.*, in which she sustained the character of Queen Katherine, this lady took her leave of the Marylebone Theatre, on Monday, the 8th of May. Mrs. Warner had to confess the failure of her efforts to create an audience, and pecuniarily she was a heavy loser by her speculation, but in an artistic sense she had covered herself with glory, and her experiment, so honourably conceived, and to the end so consistently carried out, will ever remain a memorable feature in the chronicles of the English stage.

After continuing closed for some weeks, the house was reopened by Mr. Walter Watts, in the middle of July, with Mr. and Mrs. Keeley in Bayle Bernard's romantic drama, *Lucille, a Tale of the Heart*. Mr. Watts began by managing on the starring system, but his stars were supported by a good working company, and the same careful attention was bestowed upon all the embellish-

ments of the stage, as during the reign of Mrs. Warner.
If there was not the same continuous design, there was
still enough of merit, and elegance, in the performances,
to retain the *prestige* already gained. The Keeleys
remained for some weeks, playing in *The Dream at Sea*,
Martin Chuzzlewit, *The Forty Thieves*, and other of their
old Lyceum pieces, and were succeeded by the Irish
comedian, Mr. Hudson; by the Americans, Mr. Davenport and Mrs. Mowatt, the latter an actress of more
sweetness than power, endowed with rare personal love-
liness and charm; and by Mr. T. P. Cooke, who, of
course, brought with him *The Pilot*, *Poor Jack*, and the
inevitable *Black-Eyed Susan*. A one-act drama, which
still lives, *The Midnight Watch*, by Mr. Maddison Mor-
ton, first saw the light here in October, and was very well
acted by Miss Fanny Vining, Mr. H. T. Craven, and Mr.
James Johnstone. Early in November, Mr. Buckstone
and Mrs. Fitzwilliam commenced, with *The Flowers of the
Forest*, an engagement which lasted for the remainder of
the year.

Mr. Davenport and Mrs. Mowatt returned at the beginning of 1849, and the management then settled down to
a steady course, relying upon the production of the Modern, in conjunction with the Elder, Drama. The company, in addition to the above, consisted of the Misses
Fanny Vining, Villars, M. Oliver, and Charlotte Saunders;
Mrs. Newberry and Mrs. Johnstone; Messrs. James
Johnstone, H. T. Craven, Belton, George Cooke, Herbert,
Norton, and J. W. Ray. "A new and original five-act
drama" of the picturesque and romantic school, entitled,

Armand, or the Peer and the Peasant, of which Mrs. Mowatt herself was the authoress, was the first event of the new year. Tobin's delightful comedy, *The Honeymoon*, was given in February, with Mr. Davenport as Duke Aranza, Mrs. Mowatt as Juliana, and Miss Vining as Donna Volante. Mr. Watts also produced *A Dream of Life*, written by himself, at the end of March, and Mr Benjamin Barnett appeared as Monsieur Jacques, in his brother, Morris Barnett's version of Scribe's vaudeville. *Pizarro* was revived in a very creditable manner, with Mrs. Mowatt as Elvira, Miss F. Vining as Cora, and Mr. Davenport as Rolla, in March. The Easter novelties consisted of a five-act play, *The Heart's Trials*, by Mr. Hughes, of the Adelphi Theatre, followed by a burlesque on *Guy Fawkes*, written by Albert Smith. A little later Mrs. Mowatt appeared as Juliet, to the Mercutio of Mr. Davenport, and the Romeo of Miss Fanny Vining. In May, a version of Latour's tragedy, *Virginie*, adapted for the London stage, by Mr. John Oxenford, under the title of *Virginia*, was brought out for Mrs. Mowatt, who had seldom been seen to greater advantage. Early in June Mrs. Centlivre's comedy, *The Wonder*, was given with Miss Vining as Violante ; and a week later Mr. Henry Spicer's drama, *The Witch-Wife*—a composition of high merit—was produced, in which Mr. Ray created a marked impression as Sir Gerald Mole, and Mrs. Mowatt sustained the part of Cecil Howard with much grace and feeling. The season closed in July, with a performance of *Love's Sacrifice*, and the old melodrama of *Luke the Labourer*—with Mr. Johnstone's Luke—as the afterpiece.

The theatre reopened on Monday, the 17th of September, with a new tragedy, *Velasco, or Castilian Honour*, by an American author, Mr. Eps Sargent. In this Mr. Davenport, Mr. James Johnstone, Misses Vining and Oliver appeared. Planché's extravaganza, *Fortunio*, was then revived on a scale of much splendour, and Mrs. Mowatt reappeared as Beatrice in *Much Ado about Nothing*. Charles Kemble's play, *The Point of Honour*, was produced for Mr. Davenport and Miss Vining in October; and we find O'Keefe's old musical farce, *The Poor Soldier*, also in the bills. A more important event was the revival of Shakspeare's *Cymbeline* at the end of this month. The *ensemble* was found unsatisfactory, but Mrs. Mowatt was an ideal Imogene. A new drama, *The Crusaders*, by a Mr. J. Ebsworth, written chiefly in blank verse, was given with success eaily in November, and Planché's *White Cat* succeeded *Fortunio*, as the after-piece. During the last weeks of the same month the excellent acting of Mrs. Mowatt as Neighbour Constance, and the richness of the decorations, gave considerable importance to the representation of Sheridan Knowles's *Love Chase*. The final "circumstance" of Mr. Watts' management was the revival of *Twelfth Night*, in which Mr. Davenport played Malvolio to the Viola of Mrs. Mowatt. The season terminated on Monday, the 10th of December, the piece chosen for the occasion being Knowles's *Wife of Mantua*, in which Mrs. Mowatt played Mariana, and Mr. Davenport St. Pierre. Mr. Watts [1] removed to the New Olympic

---

[1] A few months later Mr. Watts, who was a clerk in the Globe Insurance Office, was arrested on a charge of defalca-

Theatre at Christmas, as offering a wider field of enterprise, and the Marylebone was sublet to Mr. Edward
Stirling.

Mr. Stirling commenced operations on Boxing-night
with a pantomime, *Harlequin Fairy-Land,* the joint
invention of Mr. Walter Watts and Mr. Nelson Lee. This
was followed by a series of his own dramas, such as
*Nicholas Nickleby, The Mendicant's Son, The Road of
Life, Jane Lomax,* and others, all of the "domestic" order,
in which Mrs. Gordon took the lead.   At Easter, 1850,
Mr. Gustavus Brooke was engaged for a series of Shakspearian performances, supported by Messrs. James Johnstone, Belton, Herbert, and Mrs. Seymour. In the middle
of November Mr. Joseph Stammers, the well-known
entrepreneur of the once popular Wednesday concerts,
became lessee, and brought with him the charming Mrs.
Nisbett, who, as Lady Gay Spanker, Neighbour Constance, and Helen in *The Hunchback,* delighted the inhabitants of Marylebone, but showed the limit of her powers
by attempting Portia—to the Shylock of Mr. James
Johnstone.   There was an excellent pantomime, *Harlequin Alfred the Great, or the Magic Raven and the
Mystic Banjo,* from the pen of Mr. George Herbert Rodwell, at Christmas, with Tom Matthews as Clown.   Mr.
Stammers dignified his theatre with the imposing title of
the "London English Opera." The only pieces given,
however, with even the slightest lyric pretension, were the
old musical dramas of *Rob Roy* and *The Slave,* and per-

tion, and died shortly afterwards, by his own hand, in
prison.

haps Shakspeare's *Macbeth*, with Locke's choruses, and Mr. Henry Drayton as Hecate.

The house closed rather suddenly at the beginning of February, 1851, and Mr. Stammers was made a bankrupt. The name of Mr. E. T. Smith next appeared at the head of the announcements, in the autumn of this year. This venture was, we believe, the beginning of a managerial career, which, extending over the next twenty years, or more, included in its course at least six of the metropolitan houses, besides the gardens of Vauxhall, Cremorne, and Highbury Barn. Mr. Smith led off with English operas, supported by Mr. and Mrs. Donald King, Mr. Henry Drayton, Mr. Gregg, Mr. Frazer, Mr. Lawler, Miss Lanza, and Miss Helen Condell, all names of a certain note in the musical world of that day. Mr. N. T. Hicks and transpontine melodrama were then tried. At Easter, 1852, he sublet the property to Mr. George Bolton, who got up a very fair revival of *The Tempest*, for the holiday-makers, and subsequently engaged the eminent tragedian, Mr. James Anderson, for a short series of performances, after which Mr. Smith himself resumed the cares of management, and introduced, as Sir Giles Overreach, Mr. McKean Buchanan, an American, whose style, though not without merit, was marred by an extravagance, which prevented him from securing a definite position on the London boards. During Mr. Buchanan's engagement, which lasted for some months, Shiel's old tragedy *The Apostate, or the Moors in Spain*, was unearthed. This play had been rendered famous at Covent Garden in 1817, by the

H 2

talents of Charles Kemble, Young, Egerton, and Miss
O'Neil, in combination. As might be imagined, it
scarcely caused any excitement now. Mr. Smith's
system of management was certainly not an elevated
one, yet he contrived, nevertheless, from time to time,
to present some very good acting to his patrons. In
addition to Mr. Buchanan, Mr. James Rogers and Mrs.
Brougham played in 1852. Charles Freer was here at
Easter, 1853, and was followed by Mr. Davenport, Mr.
Charles Selby, Mr. T. Mead, and Miss Fanny Vining.
Amongst the plays selected at various times, we find John
Wilkins' admirable *Civilization*, and Mrs. Lovell's no less
admirable *Ingomar*, in addition to the time-honoured
melodramas of *The Tower of Nêsle*, *The Red Rover*, and
The Innkeeper of Abbeville, not to forget another, newer,
and yet more thrilling in its denomination, *The Assassin
Monk, or the Sentinel of the Thirteenth Chime !!!*

In the autumn of 1853, Mr. E. T. Smith removed to
the larger field of Drury Lane, and the Marylebone
Theatre passed into the hands of Mr. J. William Wallack, an actor favourably known to the London public
by his performances of the Shaksperian drama a year or
two previously at the Haymarket. It was evidently the
aim of Mr. Wallack to regain for the house, if possible,
the position which it had held under the direction of
Mr. Watts and Mrs Warner. For this purpose he engaged a company comprising, besides himself and Mrs.
Wallack, an actress of no mean ability, the names of
Messrs. Henry Vandenhoff, George Cooke, J. W. Shalders,
Edgar, F. Charles, C. Bender, Clinton, and W. Wallis ;

Misses Harriet Gordon, Fanny Garthwaite, Emily Horton, and Mrs. Robertson. On the opening night, early in October, the old comedy, *A Cure for the Heartache*, and Planché's extravaganza, *The Fair One with the Golden Locks*, were represented, and to these succeeded *Speed the Plough*, *Abelard and Heloise*, and John Daly's drama, *Broken Toys*. On Wednesday, the 19th of October, Mr. and Mrs. Wallack made their first appearance as the Thane and his wife, in a very carefully got-up revival of *Macbeth*. *The Stranger*, *Othello*, *The Bridal*—in which Mrs. Wallack as Evadne, and her husband as Melantius, created a powerful impression—and *The Lady of Lyons* followed. Colley Cibber's version of *King Richard III.* was given in November, with Mr. Wallack as Glo'ster, and Mr. Henry Vandenhoff as Richmond. Miss Julia Harland was added to the *corps*, for the after-pieces, upon which much attention was bestowed by the management. Among the more prominent of these were Francis Talfourd's burlesque, *Alcestis*, Gay's *Beggar's Opera*, and the old burletta *Midas*. A new farce by Mr. Albany Fonblanque, entitled *Metempsychosis ; or, Which is Which ?* was also brought out. Of other revivals we may notice *The Honeymoon*, and Maturin's now forgotten and gloomy tragedy of *Bertram*, originally written for Edmund Kean, in which Mrs. Wallack electrified her audience as Imogen. There was a very good pantomime at Christmas, *Harlequin King Ugly-Mug, and my Lady Lee, of Old London Bridge*, written by Mr. Nelson Lee. The clown was Paul Kellino. Mr. and Mrs. Wallack reappeared in *Pizarro* at the beginning of February, 1854, and immediately afterwards Judge Talfourd's *Ion* was produced with new and elaborate scenery and costumes. Mrs. Wallack added greatly to her laurels as Ion, and the Adrastus of Mr. Wallack also met with general approbation. On the alternate evenings Byron's *Werner* was given, with similar attention to the stage appointments. A version of the French spectacular drama, *La Prière des Naufrages*, which, as *The Thirst of Gold*, had already made a considerable sensation at the Adelphi, was brought out at the end of February under the title of *The Struggle for Gold, and the Orphan of the Frozen Sea.* This was chiefly remarkable for the magnificence of the mounting, and for the highly picturesque manner in which Mrs. Wallack supported the character of the Indian girl. A revival, also with new scenery and dresses, of *Romeo and Juliet*, was to be noticed for the Romeo of Mrs. Wallack, the Mercutio of Mr. Wallack, and for the *début*, as Juliet, of Miss Cleveland, now best known as the accomplished actress and polished elocutionist, Mrs. Arthur Stirling. Mr. Hoskins, from Sadler's Wells, was engaged at Easter to play in *Clari, the Maid of Milan*, reproduced with Sir Henry Bishop's songs and glees. The holiday programme was supplemented by a fairy extravaganza, *The Magic Branch*, from the pen of a new and competent author, Mr. Collis. In this Mr. Shalders distinguished himself in the twofold capacity of comedian and scene-painter, whilst Miss Harriet Gordon and Mr. George Cooke completed the effect by their excellent singing and acting. Mr. Eliot Galer, Mr. Henry Drayton, and Miss Susannah Lowe subsequently gave a few performances of English opera, with an orchestra and chorus directed by the composer, Mr. John Francis Duggan. The legitimate drama was then resumed with *William Tell*, *Virginius*, *The Hunchback*, *The Love Chase*, *Jane Shore*, *The Wonder*, *The Wife*, and *The School of Reform*, presented in rapid succession, and a season both honourable and remunerative to the management came to its conclusion at the end of the month of May.

Encouraged by his well-merited success, Mr. William Wallack issued a circular to the patrons of the Marylebone Theatre, previous to the commencement of his second season. In this he promised many alterations and improvements, a stage lengthened—by the removal of a back wall—to the depth of 115 feet, and an elegant re-decoration in every part of the interior. More interesting still, however, was his expressed purpose of providing "a home for the highest Drama of England," and of encouraging "to the utmost, the living proofs and witnesses of its indestructible genius." Not only were the plays of Shakspeare and the old dramatists to be presented, with every attainable appliance of scenic and decorative art, but "new and original dramas" were, from time to time, to be introduced, and mounted with the same care and cost. "Justice," added the lessee, "will be done to the living, as to the dead; and no means left unattempted to raise the Victorian age, in its dramatic relations, to a level with the Elizabethan era." The tone of this preamble was perhaps grandiloquent, but there was nevertheless an honest purpose, honestly fulfilled, beyond.

Eventually the Marylebone reopened on Saturday, the 7th of October, with a revival of *As You Like It*, strictly in accordance with the text of Shakspeare, and profusely illustrated with new and beautiful scenery, painted by Mr. Shalders, together with costumes of a novel and picturesque design. An overture, *entr'actes*, and some incidental music were also composed by Mr. J. F. Duggan, who himself presided in the orchestra. Mrs. Wallack's Rosalind astonished those who had hitherto only seen her in such parts as Lady Macbeth, and was played throughout with a gaiety, and youthfulness, which literally left nothing to criticize. Mrs. Wallack received much graceful support from the Celia of Miss Cleveland. Orlando was neatly rendered by Mr. Edgar, and the Jacques of Mr. William Wallack proved a very fine specimen of elocutionary power. The other parts were respectably filled, and the whole gave unqualified satisfaction to a crowded and brilliant audience.

As regarded the new and original dramas promised in the introductory address, it was soon understood that the lessee had accepted three hitherto unacted plays, the respective claims of which would be tested as speedily as possible. The first of these, *Videna*, a drama in five acts, founded on a legend in Geoffrey of Monmouth, and written by Mr. John A. Heraud, was given on Monday, the 23rd of October. The subject was found overcharged with horrors, and the action, especially in the last two acts, to be impeded by the dialogue, which was much too verbose; but, thanks to the very fine acting of the Wallacks and Miss Cleveland, and to the beauty of the mounting, the play—in itself by no means devoid of interest—obtained a certain measure of success. The second, *Love and Loyalty*, by Mr. Robson, was tried on Monday, the 13th of November. The scene of this play was laid in the reign of Charles II., and contained one very effective and poetical situation. This was where the hero, Marston, son of a cavalier who had fallen at Naseby, returns to his old home—now in the possession of a Roundhead, whose daughter, Juliet, he loves—and, standing on his ancestral hearth, appeals to his father's portrait, when taunted by the old man with his poverty and consequent unworthiness to be her suitor. The scenes were too prolonged, and the dialogue needed much compression, but the characters generally were drawn with considerable skill. That of Marston had a marked individuality, and, being exactly fitted to Mr. Wallack's style of acting, secured the requisite success of the piece..

The management now reverted to the old dramatists, and revived the *Venice Preserved* of Otway, in which the lessee played Jaffier, and his wife, Belvidera, with all their accustomed excellence. A new candidate for popular favour, endowed with many personal advantages, Mr. H. G. Mapleson, showed promise in the part of Pierre. Mr. Nelson Lee's Christmas pantomime, *Young Norval on the Grampian Hills*, was produced on a scale of splendour, at that time unusual in a suburban theatre, and in other respects fully answered its purpose, as a temporary source of attraction. The third of the new plays, promised at the beginning of the season, was produced early in February. This turned out to be the old story of the Man in the Iron Mask dramatized, in five acts, with much taste and skill by Mr. Bayle Bernard, under the title of *Leon of the Iron Mask*. The extreme length of the stage was made the most of by the scenic artist, Mr. Shalders, who achieved wonders in a representation of the interior of the Louvre. Shakspeare's *Winter's Tale* was revived in a very elegant and elaborate manner on Monday, the 5th of March. Much new business was introduced, and the whole revival wore an air of originality. Mr. Wallack proved very effective in the part of Leontes, and the Hermione of Mrs. Wallack was a very fine and classical performance. The statue scene was greatly applauded. This was the last "circumstance" of Mr. William Wallack's management, which terminated at the end of the month. The encouragement bestowed upon his first season was deceptive. The second showed a loss to the treasury, which left him no choice but to relinquish an undertaking which, interesting though it might be, to the better class of playgoers, had proved, in a financial sense, so utterly unproductive. His gallant effort, however, to establish a taste for the Poetic Drama in the north-west suburb of the metropolis will always remain among the most cherished traditions of the obscure little theatre in Church Street.

Mr. Henry Meadows ventured on a spring season at Easter, and in October a former lessee, Mr. John Douglass, returned to his old quarters, bringing with him Mr. Charles Freer, as stage-manager, and a rearrangement—which meant a reduction—of prices. Miss Edith

Heraud appeared as Julia in *The Hunchback*, and Mr. James Anderson played a welcome engagement, on alternate nights, with an English opera company, which included the names of George Perren and Hamilton Braham. Mr. Douglass, who was a very good actor of the T. P. Cooke type, appeared as Ben the Boatswain in February, and Miss Glyn gave a reading of *Macbeth* in March. Mr. E. C. Seaman next leased the house at Easter, 1856, with a company containing the worthy names of Mr. Stuart, Mr. Belford, Mr. Lewis Ball, Miss Anderton, and Miss Hughes—now Mrs. Gaston Murray. Mr. Charles Mathews and Miss Fitzpatrick were playing at different times in April, and Mr. and Mrs. Leigh Murray, Mr. Edward and Mr. Gaston Murray, Flexmore, Sam Cowell, and Miss Wadham assisted at Miss Hughes' benefit on the 24th of that month. The enterprise having turned out a failure, Mr. Seaman was replaced by a Mr. Bigwood. During June we find artists like Miss Glyn, Miss Oliver, and Mr. James Johnstone lending their services for benefits, but, generally speaking, the entertainments just now were of a very uninteresting description. Mr. James Anderson again " starred," in conjunction with Miss Agnes Elsworthy, for a week in September, and Mr. Bigwood retired from the direction at Michaelmas. The theatre remained closed till Boxing-night, when it was reopened by the well-known actor, Mr. Emery, with Shirley Brooks's drama, *The Creole*, and a pantomime, *Tit, Tat, Toe*, by Francisco Frost. Buck-stone's *Isabelle* was revived early in January, 1857, with Miss Clifford from the Princess's in the title *rôle*, and a domestic drama, *Ruth Oakley*, by Messrs. Harris and Williams, with a plot resembling in many particulars that of Kotzebue's *Stranger*, was produced, in which Mr. Emery's rough, but natural acting, as a blacksmith, created some attention. A version of *Uncle Tom's Cabin* served to introduce Miss Cordelia Howard, an American child-actress of much aptitude, as Eva. An amateur, Sir William Don, made his first appearance in London as the Bailie, in *Rob Roy*, in March. Mr. Emery's tenancy, though meritorious, was not more prosperous than those of his predecessors, and the Marylebone again changed hands at Easter, this time opening under Mr. Edgar, and Mr. Elliston, with *The Marble Heart.* Mrs. Emma Waller played Pauline, in *The Lady of Lyons*, for the benefit of the latter, on Monday, June the 16th. Mr. and Mrs. Clarence Holt made a praiseworthy fight for legitimacy, with rather limited resources, in the ensuing winter, opening with Wilkins's *Civilization.* Westland Marston's *Strathmore*, and Lovell's *Provost of Bruges* were revived in January, 1858. Unfortunately, another failure had to be recorded, and early in the spring the house was once more in the market.

The fortunes of the Marylebone at this period had probably reached their lowest ebb. That the house could boast of the longest stage, and the shortest seasons, of any theatre in London, was a maxim laid down in every greenroom. As a theatrical property, the estimation in which it was held was so low, that no speculator would care to touch it. At this crisis in its fate, however, Mr. J. H. Arnold Cave stepped in, and was daring enough to try his chance, on a field which had hitherto proved fatal to so many.   Commencing his season on Whit-Monday, the 25th of May, 1858, he managed to keep open house for upwards of two years, without once closing its doors.   That the Marylebone Theatre now took high ground, or that it did much for art, cannot with truth be said.   But it may, at any rate, be conceded that Mr. Cave succeeded in paying his way, and that,— better still,—he succeeded in making *his way pay him.* The nightly programme, at first, was that of a mere theatre of varieties, and based on the music-hall principle, but gradually the drama—such as it was—again predominated, and, later on, actors of acknowledged reputation could, now and again, be seen here.   Mr. George Belmore, and Mr. Henry Forrester, then mere beginners, about this date worked their way to the front, on these boards.   Mr. Townshend, formerly member for Greenwich, essayed to play Shylock, with the aid of Miss Anderton as Portia, in November of this year, and at Christmas Mr. Frederick Fenton painted the scenery for Mr. Hazlewood's pantomime of *Goody Goose*, in which the lessee filled the part of Greenheart.   Mr. Edward Stirling's *Aline, the Rose of Killarney; Belphegor, the Mountebank ; The Corsican Brothers;* and *Don Cæsar de Bazan* were given in the earlier months of 1859, and for Mr. Cave's benefit, on the 16th of June, the nautical drama, *My Poll and my Partner Joe*, together with Shield's old ballad opera, *Rosina*.   Sheridan Knowles's *William Tell* was tried in September, and Mr. N. T. Hicks, so famous in his own line, reappeared in November. Mr. Charles Dillon returned in the following March, and Mr. George Belmore, and Mr. W. Shalders in April. The house closed for cleaning and repairs at the end of July, but reopened in the middle of August. A very clever boy, Master Percy Roselle, subsequently remembered as the juvenile hero of *King Pippin*, and other Drury Lane pantomimes, came out in November. Mr. J. F. Young sustained the leading parts at this date. Miss Marriott enacted Romeo, Hamlet, and Rosalind in April, 1861, and Mdme. Celeste fulfilled an engagement in the July of that year, performing in *The Abbé Vaudreuil*, and in Bayle Barnard's *St. Mary's Eve.*

The most noteworthy event of 1862 was the engagement for six nights, in April, of Mr. Benjamin Webster, and Mr. Paul Bedford, for whom Watts Phillipps's celebrated play, *The Dead Heart*, was got up. Miss Mandlebert, a once favourite actress, was to be seen here in the pantomime at Christmas. Mr. Arthur Stirling appeared in *Macbeth*, and *Hamlet*, during Passion Week, 1863, and Toole played for Mr. Cave's benefit on Wednesday, the 1st of April, as did also Mr. Belmore—now established as an actor of celebrity, at the West End, by his remarkable creation of Stephen Hargreaves, the "Softy," in a dramatic version of Miss Braddon's novel, *Aurora Floyd*, at the Princess's Theatre.

We may briefly dispose of the remaining events in Mr. Cave's management, which terminated about Easter, 1867. Moncrieffe's *Claude Duval* was revived in May, 1863. Mr. Benjamin Webster accepted another engagement for six nights in the November of that year, and on

Christmas Eve the since celebrated Vokes family made their first bow to a London public in the pantomime, *Harlequin Jack Frost*. Mr. Henry Lorraine was here in March, and Mr. Belmore in September, 1864. An Australian actor, Mr. Neil Warner, had some success as Hamlet and Shylock in March, 1865. Mr. Henry Neville, Mr. H. J. Montague, Miss Lydia Foote, and Miss Nellie Farren gave their services in Tom Taylor's *Ticket-of-Leave Man* for Mr. Cave's benefit, during July, 1866. Mr. Felix Rogers, a burlesque actor of repute, superintended the direction, whilst the lessee went over to Sadler's Wells in August. Mr. James Anderson was once more engaged in December, and produced his own play—of very considerable merit—*The Scottish Chief*, in which Miss Ada Cavendish sustained the part of Helen Mar. Mr. T. Thorne also played on one occasion, for a benefit, at this date. *The Dog of Montargis* was revived in March, 1867. Miss Augusta Thomson starred in April, as well as Mr. Walter Montgomery, Miss Fanny Addison, and Miss Atkinson from Drury Lane. Mr. Cave, being engaged to direct the stage arrangements of the Victoria Palace Theatre, sub-let the Marylebone, at Whitsuntide, to Miss Augusta Thomson, and a Miss Estelle Bodenham, who opened with the *Beggars' Opera*. Mr. Henry Lorraine, Mr. Edmund Phelps, and Miss Hudspeth were members of the company during their brief tenure, which expired in August. Mr. Albert Montgomery, and Mr. Clifford Lacy, held it successively during the winter. Mr. Charles Verner was their principal actor, and played, in conjunction with Mr. Arnold Cave, and Miss Mary Marshall—ranked in her day among the best of stage *soubrettes*—for Mr. Lacy's benefit in July, 1868.

Early in the autumn of this year it was rumoured that the Marylebone had found a new proprietor, who intended to raise the prices, and restore it to the level of a first-class theatre. Accordingly, on Saturday, the 10th of October, having been very handsomely re-decorated and re-christened the "Royal Alfred," in compliment to H.R.H. the Duke of Edinburgh—who was present during the evening—it was opened, with some ceremony, under the lesseeship of Mr. H. R. Lacey, and the stage direction of the well-known actress, Miss Amy Sedgwick. The lessee delivered an inaugural address, in which he spoke of "throwing sensation to the winds," and "devoting his theatre to high-class comedy." His speech was scarcely borne out by the performance, which consisted of a new drama of "strong interest," by Mr. C. H. Stephenson, entitled *Pindee Singh*, in which Mr. Neil Warner, Mr. George Melville, Mrs. Stephens, Miss C. Forde, and Miss Amy Sedgwick appeared, followed by a very broad farce, *The Goose with the Golden Eggs*. Mr. Lacey's efforts did not meet with the support anticipated, and the speculation was abandoned at the end of a month. Mr. Lacey made a second attempt, with a pantomime, *Whittington and his Cat*, at Christmas, and on the termination of its run at the end of February, 1867, gave way to Miss Henrade, who opened on Easter Monday with Boucicault's *Flying Scud*. Mr. Worboys, Mr. Charles Harcourt, and Mr. George Sidney, then tried their hands at management in succession, without much result. Miss Rosina Ranoe played in the opening of Mr. Soutar's pantomime, *Gulliver's Travels*, towards the close of 1869. Mr. Giovanelli, who had recently relinquished the direction of Highbury Barn, occupied the house in the winter of 1870-71, and had a benefit in March of the latter year, at which Miss Fanny Huddart, and Miss Rebecca Isaacs, Messrs. Alfred Rayner, McIntyre, Fairclough, C. Seyton, and George Honey, assisted.

Mr. Giovanelli was succeeded at Easter, 1871, by Mr. Charles Harcourt, who opened with *The Colleen Bawn*, and Burnand's burlesque, *Black-Ey'd Susan*, in which Miss M. Oliver, and Mr. Dewar, appeared. The Alfred Theatre, as it was still called, seemed now to assume a better position than for a long time past. The well-known tragedian, Mr. T. Swinbourne, was engaged for first lead, and a series of Shakspearian representations, including *Othello*, *Macbeth*, and *Hamlet*, were very creditably put upon the stage. As the summer advanced, the performances assumed a lighter character. *The Flowers of the Forest*, *The Streets of London*, *Gilderoy*, and Watts Phillipps's *Nobody's Child*, were consecutively found in the bills. The Gaiety company, comprising Miss Julia Matthews and Miss Albertazzi, Messrs. J. D. Stoyle, Aynsley Cook, and J. G. Taylor, played in opera-bouffe. Miss Henrietta Hodson, a very talented and popular actress, was also here, and a sensational drama, *Across the Continent*, by an American author—Mr. James McCloskey—made a decided hit in July. In October, Shakspeare's *King John* was mounted, on a really superior

I

scale, and its principal characters were very adequately interpreted by a new actor, Mr. Pennington, Mr. and Mrs. Charles Harcourt, and their company. A new drama by Mr. Burnand, *Paul Zegers, or the Dream of Retribution*—for the leading part of which Mr. Marcus Elmore was specially engaged—was brought out in November. This play might well bear revival at theatres of greater pretension. Later, there was a good pantomime, *The House that Jack Built*, and a good clown, Harry Paulo. Another new play, *A Life's Race*, written by a Miss Evelyn, was given about the middle of February, 1872, and acted by the authoress, in conjunction with Mr. and Mrs. Harcourt, Mr. Swinbourne, and that consummate artist, Mr. Herman Vezin. Mr. Swinbourne also played Sir Edward Mortimer, in *The Iron Chest*, and, on the 16th of March, Mr. Lionel Brough gave his services for the benefit of Mr. Harcourt, whose term had now expired. Miss Nelson made a brief experiment in management during the following winter, and on Whit-Monday, 24th of May, 1873, Mr. Arnold Cave once more resumed his old place as lessee, with the clever and fascinating Miss Litton as "star" for the opening representations.

Mr. Cave, at first alone, and afterwards with Mr. Albert West as partner, has, down to the present time, retained the lesseeship of the Marylebone Theatre, which speedily resumed its original nomenclature. He has conducted it entirely as a low-priced theatre, for the entertainment of the masses; and the duration of his management is the best proof of its success, and of the approbation with which it is regarded by the neighbour-

hood.   Appealing solely to one class of frequenters, and
those of a very humble description, splendour on either
side of the footlights was neither practicable, nor to be
looked for.   Yet the house, nevertheless, has been respectably conducted ; and, occasionally, actors of position
have trod its boards.   Mr. T. C. King had an engagement in June, 1873.   Mr. Belmore, Mr. Emery, and Mr.
Alfred Rayner were more than once performing here ;
and Mr. Creswick played a round of Shakspearian parts
in December, 1876.   For the rest, *The Crimes and
Cruelties of Mother Brownrigg, The Mysterious House at
Chelsea, Steelcap the Robber,* and " the interesting slave-
drama," *Ida May,* have happily been relieved by plays
of a worthier class, like *All that glitters is not Gold,
Marianne, the Child of Charity*—an old and well-con-
structed domestic drama, written for the Victoria in the
days of Miss Vincent—and Halliday's *King of Scots.*   It is
curious, moreover, to note that within the last ten years,
pieces so venerable in their antiquity as the pantomime
of *Mother Goose, Don Giovanni in London, Tom and
Jerry, The Scamps of London,* and *Therese, the Orphan of
Geneva,* together with those dearly-loved favourites of our—
and our grandsires'—childhood, *The Miller and his Men,
The Castle Spectre, The Knight and the Wood-Demon,* and,
above all others, *Raymond and Agnes, or the Bleeding
Nun of Lindenberg* have, at intervals, been given at
the Marylebone Theatre.   Clearly, then, our manager
possesses classical inclinations, which, under other conditions, might have developed themselves into something
more elevating than the above.   But Mr. Cave is con-

trolled by the exigencies of his situation, and, wise in his generation, provides for his audiences such fare as seems most likely to answer the purpose of both.   As a liberal, and very kind-hearted man, and as the prosperous proprietor of an institution, erstwhile the scene of such innumerable misfortunes, he deservedly stands high in the estimation of his neighbours; and that he may long continue to remain " the right man in the right place " is, without doubt, the wish of all who know him. Should the Marylebone, however, " in the whirligig of time" fall into other hands, and sufficient capital be forthcoming for the implanting of a purer taste, in a quarter which boasts—be it known—its wealthier, as well as its poorer inhabitants, such an enterprise, whatever the result, would at any rate not be opening up entirely new ground.   For we believe we have shown, in the foregoing sketch, that there have been periods in its earlier career, when more than one brave and protracted fight was made for the establishment of the highest forms of the drama, both new and old, in the lowly little playhouse overshadowed by—Portmar Market.

"THREE LYCEUMS."

THE present Lyceum Theatre, in Wellington Street, Strand—the third standing upon the same site—owes its origin to a building erected in 1765, by the well-known architect, James Payne, on some ground belonging to the old town-house of the Lords Exeter. It was originally intended for a Picture Gallery, and the "Incorporated Society of British Artists" at first held their annual exhibition here. But the Lyceum also, in its earlier existence, seems to have been turned to many other uses. In the winter of 1783, Signor Biaggini exhibited an air balloon, described as "an Aerostatical Globe of ten feet in diameter, at the Great Room, known by the name of Lyceum, nearly opposite Somerset House, Strand." In the following February, the Montgolfier balloon was shown "for a few days, before its removal to Oxford, in the Grand Apartment called the Lyceum, three doors above Exeter Change." This balloon, we are told, was forty feet in circumference, was entirely overlaid with gold, and was exhibited by a Monsieur Chevalier. Other balloons were also shown, by Lunardi, and Count Zambeccari, during this same year. They were followed, in 1785, by an exhibition of waxwork, quaintly set forth, in the phraseology of that day, as "a Cabinet of Royal Figures, most curiously moulded in wax, as large as Nature." The visitors to this exhibition were further informed that they might have their portraits taken, in wax, or miniature, by the proprietor of the show, and " should the Portraits not be thought the most striking and correct Likenesses, he would not expect anything for his trouble." This was at any rate honest on the part of the proprietor—a certain Mr. Sylvester.

Collins gave a comic musical lecture, *The Evening Brush*, in the years 1788-9, when Master Linley occa sionally played the violoncello, between the parts. This young Linley was subsequently the famous violoncello player of the opera orchestra. George Savile Carey was lecturing here, in April, 1789, and in December the elder Dibdin gave his entertainment, *The Oddities, or Dame Nature in a Frolic*. Dibdin also lectured in January, 1791, and in March of that year Moses Kean, the ventri-loquist, and father—or uncle—of Edmund Kean, gave his imitations. In or about the year 1794, Dr. Arnold, the musical composer, converted the back part of the pre-mises into a small theatre—henceforth the first Lyceum Theatre—but was unable to procure a licence for theatrical performances, owing to the then all-powerful opposition of the Drury Lane and Covent Garden managers. Astley, however, burnt out in Westminster, took refuge, with his equestrian company, at the new theatre, in the months of August and September. A little earlier, Mr. Reeve had been giving his lecture, *Mirth's Museum, or the Country Club*, on the same boards. In 1795, it was opened as Handy's New Circus, with "The Little Devil" from Sadler's Wells, and other popular performers. In 1798, it was a "Theatre of Astronomy," in which Mr. Lloyd displayed his *Dio-astro-doxon, or Grand Transparent Orrery.* On Monday, the 22nd of July, 1799, Mr. Wilks, of the Dublin Theatre, delivered a lecture, *A Cabinet of Fancy*, illustrated by transparencies.

In the year 1800, Cartwright's " Musical Glasses," long a favourite amusement with the public, were to be heard at the Lyceum. During the next year, Mr. Phillipstahl set up his *Phantasmagoria ;* and in 1802, "The Invisible Girl" was the attraction. Robert Ker Porter's large pictures, The Battle of Alexandria, The Earthquake at Lisbon, The Battle of Lodi, and others, were successively shown, during the early years of the present century. An exhibition of gas illumination was the feature of 1804, and Laurent attempted what would now be styled a variety entertainment, consisting of music, dancing, and short pantomimes, the first of which latter was *Neptune, or Harlequin Woodcutter*, in 1805. The first play ever acted on the stage of the original Lyceum Theatre was, we believe, Otway's once famous, but now almost forgotten tragedy, *Venice Preserved.* This was represented by some amateurs, on Monday, the 21st of April, 1806, under the special patronage and countenance of the Duchess of Gordon, one of the best-known leaders of society, at the time. Robert Palmer gave his *Portraits of the Living and the Dead*, in August, and the singer, Incledon, his *Voyage to India*, in September of the above year. Mr. Ingleby, "the king of all the conjurors," leased the Lyceum, for the Christmas holidays of 1807-8, and in March, Dibdin introduced a new vocal entertainment, *The Professional Volunteers.* Mr. Ingleby was again here, in December, 1808, as well as for the early months of the ensuing year. His advertisement that "constant fires are kept in the theatre," would scarcely be an inducement to attract visitors in the present days of fire-panic, predominating in every place of public gathering.

The element of fire, however, indirectly exercised a very material influence upon the fortunes of the Lyceum, about this time.[1] The burning of Drury Lane Theatre —on the 24th of February, 1809, left the manager and

---

[1] The Beefsteak Club, founded by the harlequin, John Rich, in 1735, originally held its weekly meetings in a room at Covent Garden Theatre. When that house was burnt down, in the autumn of 1808, it was at first removed to the Bedford Coffee-house, in the Piazza, and ultimately, in 1809, to the Lyceum. Here it remained, until the destruction of the second Lyceum Theatre, by fire, in 1830, when its quarters were again compulsorily shifted to the coffee-house in the Piazza. After the reconstruction of the Lyceum, a *suite* of rooms were built for its accommodation under the same roof, and in these the Club was installed in 1838, and continued to occupy them, until the final dissolution of the Society in 1867. The name of William Hogarth appears amongst the original twenty-four members, and from a long list of celebrities who subsequently joined it we may single out Theophilus Cibber, in 1739; John Wilkes, in 1754; William Savage, in 1759; and Samuel Johnson, in 1780. Amongst the many distinguished members at various times, after the Club had settled in the Strand, were their Royal Highnesses the Prince of Wales (afterwards George IV.), the Duke of York, and the Duke of Sussex; also the late Duke of Leinster;

his company, on a sudden, without a home. It was willingly enough that Mr. Wroughton, and the committee, now seconded the efforts of Mr. Samuel John Arnold—son of the former proprietor—to obtain a licence for the Lyceum, since, although this only extended to the performance of operas, and the lighter forms of the drama, such as spectacle, pantomime, and extravaganza, for a limited number of weeks in each year, an arrangement could now very easily be come to, for its occupation, during the remaining months, by " Their Majesties' servants," until the larger house in Brydges Street could be rebuilt. Accordingly, all difficulties having been smoothed away, the theatre—enlarged, and redecorated—was opened by the Drury Lane company, on Tuesday, the

the Earls of Suffolk, Dalhousie, Bessborough, Strathmore, and Stair; Lord Brougham, Lord Broughton, Lord Methuen, Lord Saltoun, Sir Francis Burdett, Sir John Hales, Mr. W. H. Whitbread, M.P., Alderman Wood, Colonel Webster, Colonel Foley, Mr. W. J. Denison ; John Kemble; Lonsdale, the painter ; William Linley, the composer ; Mr. Samuel John Arnold, proprietor of the theatre ; Robert Liston ; R. B. Peake ; the well-known Mr. Henry Frederick Stephenson, long Treasurer and Secretary of the Club ; its Bard, Charles Morris, who was still a member, in 1835, at the age of ninety; his successor to the post of Bard, Charles William Hallett ; Messrs. Barrington-Bradshaw, John Trevanion, Campbell (of Islay), Riversdale Grenfell, Stewart Marjoribanks, James Hope Vere, J. R. Bulwer, Edward Tredcroft, Henry Robarts, Walter Arnold, &c. The last-named member has for ever perpetuated the manners and customs, the glories and lyrics, of the defunct Club, in his interesting volume, *The Life and Death of the Sublime Society of Beef Steaks.*

11th of April, with Colman's comedy *John Bull*, followed by the farce of *The Prize.* These were supported by Messrs Siddons, Bannister, Johnstone, Miss Duncan, and Mrs. Henry Siddons. On the next night, Elliston played Captain Absolute, to the Lydia Languish of Miss Duncan. *The Soldier's Daughter, The West Indian, The Cabinet*—with Braham, and Mrs. Mountain—*The Honeymoon, The Heir-at-Law*, a new comedy, *Grieving's a Folly*, which had had a run of several consecutive nights, *The Poor Gentleman, Three, and the Deuce, The Critic, Pizarro, The School for Scandal, Love in a Village, Rosina, Ella Rosenberg*, and *The Stranger*, were presented during the brief season which terminated on Monday, the 12th of June. On Monday, the 26th of June, the Lyceum was reopened, on his own account, by Mr. Arnold, as the English Opera House, by which name it long continued to be known. The opening novelty was a new ballad opera, *Up all Night, or the Smuggler's Cave*, composed by a Mr. King, with Dowton, Phillips, Horn, Mrs. Bishop, and Mrs. Mountain, in the principal parts. There was also a ballet, *Love in a Tub*, with music by Bishop. The scenery for both pieces was painted by Mr. Greenwood, the well-known scenic artist. The Princess of Wales,[2] who seems to have greatly affected this theatre, was present on the occasion. Various novelties were produced in the course of the season, the most noticeable amongst them being a three-act musical piece by Theodore Hook, entitled *Safe and Sound*, the cast of which

[2] Afterwards Queen Caroline, wife of George IV.

included Dowton, Horn, Phillips, Oxberry, Penson,
Smith, Wewitzer, Mrs. Mountain, Mrs. Bishop, and Mrs.
Orger. Mrs. Billington appeared as Mandane, in *Artaxerxes*, for Mrs. Mountain's benefit, on Monday, the
·11th of September, and Mr. Arnold's first season terminated most auspiciously, about a week later.

Although Mr. Arnold's licence only extended to the
summer months, the Drury Lane company, as previously
arranged, occupied it in the winter, commencing their
season on Monday, the 25th of September, and terminating
it on the 1st of June, 1810. On the first night Sheridan's
Duenna was performed, followed by *The Mayor of Garrett*,
in which Dowton and Miss Harriet Mellon—afterwards
successively Mrs. Coutts, and Duchess of St. Albans—
played. In October we find Wroughton and Miss Duncan, playing Mr. and Mrs. Oakley, in *The Jealous Wife*,
and Wrench, the excellent comedian from the Bath and
York Theatres, making his first bow to a London public,
as Belcour, in the *The West Indian*. Mrs. Edwin, with
a figure styled symmetry itself, and Knight, also made
their *débuts* in the same month, as the Widow Cheerley,
and Timothy Quaint, in *The Soldier's Daughter*. The
three new-comers made a most favourable impression, and
in conjunction with the delightful Miss Duncan, Misses
Ray and Kelly, Mrs. Orger, Mrs. Powell, and Mrs.
Sparks, Messrs. Dowton, Mathews, Raymond, De Camp,
&c., well sustained the reputation of Drury Lane, in
comedy. Tragedy was scarcely attempted, indeed the
company, as then organized, was unequal to it. Consequently a revival of Monk Lewis's *Adelgitha*, early in

1810, proved a melancholy failure, one of the performers, Mr. De Camp, appearing to such disadvantage, and being so stormily received, in the character of Lothair, that he thought proper to address the audience, and to inform them that he had not assumed the part from choice, but had had it forced upon him by the management. Such a proceeding would be scarcely put up with, in any metropolitan theatre of pretension now. Massinger's noble play *The City Madam*, altered and adapted by Sir James Burges, under the new title of *Riches, or the Wife and the Brother*, was produced in February, 1810, with Mr. Raymond as Luke; Powell, Sir John Frugal—here Traffic; Mrs. Edwin as Lady Traffic; Miss Ray and Mrs. Orger as the daughters. The play was repeated for fourteen nights, but the alterations, on the whole, were very far from improvements, though a success was at the time obtained. The play was much better done, and the original title retained, by Mr. Phelps and Mrs. Warner, many years afterwards, at Sadler's Wells.

In March a musical piece, *The Maniac*, attributed to Mr. Arnold, was brought out for Mrs. Mountain and Mrs. Bland. This had a considerable run at the time, and became, for some years after, a favourite stock-play, both in town and the provinces. The winter season came to a close with a revival of *As You Like It*, on the 1st of June, but the house was reopened, almost immediately, for the English Opera Season, with Miss Kelly as Madge, in Bickerstaff's *Love in a Village*. The doings of the English Opera, this summer, were without importance, the most interesting event being the return of Braham, who sung in *The Haunted Tower*, and other favourite

pieces, during a brief engagement in August. The Drury
Lane company, strengthened by the accession of Mrs.
Glover, and of a new comedian from Bath, a Mr. Lovegrove, returned for the winter, in the third week of Sep-
tember, and remained till the middle of June, 1811. Mrs.
Glover made her first appearance at the Lyceum, as Mrs.
Oakley, on Friday, the 28th of September, and Mr.
Lovegrove came out as Lord Ogleby in the following
week. Mrs. Edwin maintained her position, as a most
winning and graceful actress, throughout the season,
essaying amongst other parts, Peggy, in Wycherley's
Country Girl, to the Moody of Wroughton, the Sparkish
of Russell, and the Alethea of Mrs. Orger. Eschewing
Pantomime, the management offered a fairy spectacle,
The Magic Bride, as their Christmas novelty, on Boxing-
night. A new comedy, *Lost and Found*, by Mr. Masters,
was brought forward, with indifferent results, at the
beginning of the new year, but a musical farce, *The Bee-
hive*, with music by Horn, and characters by Mathews,
Wrench, Lovegrove, Mrs. Mountain, and Miss Kelly, deservedly fared much better. A little later on, Braham,
and Mrs. Bland, were to be heard, during the spring, in
The Siege of Belgrade, The Castle of Andalusia, and in a
new opera by Arnold, *The Americans*. Mathews played
Puff, and Sir Fretful Plagiary — parts, long afterwards,
doubled with equal success, by his son — for his benefit on
the 3rd of June, and the season ended on Monday,
the 18th.

Mr. Arnold's summer season of 1811 was distinguished
by more than one event of lasting interest to the lovers of
theatrical history. The first of these was the production

of an extravaganza, *The Quadrupeds, or the Manager's Last Kick.* The *Quadrupeds*—in reality a revival of Foote's mock-heroic—was meant as a satire upon the introduction of real horses—for which donkeys and mules were here substituted—in a spectacle, *Timour the Tartar*, recently mounted at Covent Garden, and which had provoked much censure from the sticklers for the legitimate. On Thursday, the 11th of August, another and more important novelty saw the light. This was Monk Lewis's long-celebrated melodrama, *One O'Clock, or the Knight and the Wood Demon*, founded on an old ballet of the same name, here expanded into three acts, with incidental songs, by King. The new play was found so long on the first night, that the audience became impatient, and the manager had to come forward, to request their forbearance, and promise curtailment. This having been effected, it was repeated on the following night, with a success which has not yet altogether died out, for *One O'Clock* may still be met with in the provinces, as well as, occasionally, at our minor metropolitan theatres, whilst its fame, as a tradition of the stage, will certainly never be effaced. Mrs. Mountain was the original Clotilda, Miss Kelly, Una, and Mrs. Bland, Paulina. The night of Monday, the 9th of September, witnessed the production of the poet Moore's solitary contribution to the stage, in the shape of a comic opera, entitled *M.P., or the Blue Stocking.* The story of this opera relates to the two sons of a Sir William Canvas, who had married their mother, at first privately, in France, but afterwards, and before the birth of the second, had gone through the ceremony publicly, in England. At his death, the younger, Charles, trusting to his brother's absence at sea, and to the difficulty of proving the first marriage, forthwith assumes the title. The scene is laid at Brighton, where also appear a French emigrant family, named De Rosier. Madame de Rosier had, it transpires, been a witness to the first marriage, consequently, the would-be Sir Charles alternately employs threats, and bribery, to suppress her testimony, but unexpectedly the elder brother returns from sea, and, establishing his claims, marries a wealthy Miss Selwyn, in whose affections his worthless brother had also, during the interim, endeavoured to supplant him. There is, in addition, an under-plot, turning upon the attachment of young De Rosier and a Miss Hartington. All, of course, ends happily, with the marriage of the four lovers. Oxberry, Horn, Raymond, Philipps, Lovegrove, Mrs. Bland, Mrs. Mountain, and Miss Kelly helped to secure the success of this little play, which Moore had made a vehicle for the introduction of some of his most captivating melodies, conspicuous amongst which were, it may be added, " Spirit of Joy," and " Farewell to the land, where in childhood I wandered," sung by Philipps, and "Young Love lived once in a humble shed," by Mrs. Bland. A most brilliant audience, including all the art-critics, and *dilettanti*, crowded the Lyceum on the first night of *M.P.*, which eventually ran, without interruption, up to the end of an unusually profitable and successful season. It will be remembered that *M.P.* was also the title adopted by the late Mr. T. W. Robertson, for the last of his comedies, produced at the Prince of Wales' Theatre, early in 1870.

Pending the reconstruction of their own theatre, the

Drury Lane comedians once more sought shelter beneath
the roof of the now popular little Lyceum, opening for
their winter season, with *The Clandestine Marriage*, on
Monday, the 23rd of September. Mrs. Edwin played
Beatrice, to the Benedick of Wrench, and Miss Duncan,
Rosalind, to the Jacques of Wroughton, at the end of
the same month. *M.P.* was also revived, cast as before,
and on one occasion *George Barnwell* was put up, with
Mrs. Glover as Millwood, and Mr. Putnam as the hero.
Braham also gave a round of his favourite characters, and
at Christmas a pantomime was produced, on the subject
of *The White Cat*, with Hartland as Harlequin, Barnes,
Pantaloon, Kirby, Clown, and pretty Miss Vallencey,
Columbine—a goodly quartet of their kind. *She Would,
and She Would Not*, was revived for Miss Duncan, in
January, 1812, and was acted twelve times in all during
the season. At the end of February, a new play, by Sir
James Burges, *The House of Morville*, "drawn," said the
bills, "in humble imitation of the ancient English Dramatists," resulted, unfortunately, in humiliating failure.
To make amends, Mrs. Le Fanu's comedy, *Prejudice,
or Modern Sentiment*, supported by Wrench, Dowton,
Johnstone, Miss Duncan, and Mrs. Edwin, was most
favourably received. For some unexplained reason, its
title was changed, on the second night, to *Sons of Erin*, a
proceeding which does not appear to have interfered with
its success. Dowton played Falstaff, in *The First Part
of King Henry IV.*, for his benefit, on Monday, the 27th
of April. A new operatic romance, by Arnold, entitled
The Devil's Bridge, with Braham, De Camp, Mrs. Bland,

and Miss Kelly, was produced on the 6th of May. *The Devil's Bridge* won a lasting popularity, and long remained one of the stock-pieces of the British Theatre. The Drury Lane company bade their final farewell to the Lyceum—henceforth, for many years, known only as the English Opera House—on the 18th of June, with a performance of Colman's *John Bull*, played gratuitously for the benefit of the English prisoners in France.

Mr. Arnold's opera seasons of 1812 and 1813 had no features of special interest. During both, novelties were of course brought out, but these, though commanding a certain vogue at the moment, had no permanent success, and were soon forgotten. In 1814, however, we find T. Cooke, Raymond, James Wallack, Pyne, Liston, Fawcett, Mrs. Orger, and Miss Kelly—a very strong array—figuring in " a new operatic anecdote," *Frederick the Great*, produced early in August. A little later, Thomas Dibdin's *Harlequin Hoax* was brought forward, with Raymond as stage-manager, Knight, the author, Patch, and Chatterley, the prompter. Both ran for several weeks, and this latter production was frequently revived here, and elsewhere. Younger playgoers may recall a modernized version of *Harlequin Hoax*, under the title, *The Manageress in a Fix, or, Please to Remember the Grotto*, provided by Mr John Oxenford, for the St. James's Theatre, whilst under Miss Herbert's direction, on Boxing-night, 1865. One more event in the season of 1814 must not go unrecorded. This was the advent of the dancer—so famous for her beauty, and for her subsequent elopement with Mr. Hughes Ball—Maria Mercandotti, to dance the

K

cachucha; and of the incomparable clown, Grimaldi, to sing Typitywichet, and to figure in a scene from *Mother Goose ;* for Fawcett's benefit, on Monday, the 15th of August. It was Grimaldi's first and only connexion with the Lyceum, for though under an engagement to Mr. Arnold some years later, illness *then* precluded him from appearing. The English Opera House reopened for the season of 1815, on Saturday, the 15th of July, with a revival of *The Devil's Bridge*, in which the great comedian, Harley—announced as "Mr. Harley, from the Theatre Royal, Brighton"—made his *début* in London, as Marcelli, and long before the evening was over, had established a position, never subsequently disputed, during a professional career of more than forty years. Mr. Harley next played Pedrillo, in *The Castle of Andalusia*, and Leatherhead, in *M.P.* Of the last-named performance, the critic of the *Morning Chronicle* wrote,—

"Mr. Harley is an actor of genuine merit. His humour is simple and unaffected. He speaks and acts from the impulse of his feelings, and imitates no predecessor in the part. He is no common candidate for public favour."

The "musical after-piece," as it was styled, of *The Maid and the Magpie*, was also produced during the season. In this, Miss Kelly drew all London to the Lyceum, by her wonderfully moving acting as Annette.

The season terminated on Friday, the 15th of September, when Mr. Raymond, the stage-manager, announced that the house would be entirely reconstructed between then, and the following summer. Mr. Raymond's speech was as follows :—

" Ladies and gentlemen, seven years have elapsed since the proprietor of the English Opera, under the immediate sanction of his Majesty, first solicited your patronage to his infant undertaking. Many were then of opinion that his attempt to establish a theatre for musical performers would end in disappointment ; but experience has proved that exertions to merit the favour of the public, are sure of their reward, and that he who labours diligently in your service, is certain to reap the gratifying harvest of your approbation. So highly does the proprietor of this theatre estimate the encouragement you have bestowed, that as a next step towards raising the character of the English opera, and establishing the undertaking on a solid basis, he means to embark on a much wider field ; and such arrangements have been made, as, he trusts, will enable him, at an early period of next summer, to greet the patrons of the present Lyceum, in an entirely new, airy, and commodious Theatre.

" He will not promise you much splendour, but he promises you the best talent which indefatigable research can procure.

" It has ever been his pride to bring forward merit to your notice, and it will ever be his boast that many of your established favourites on the larger stage, have been reared in your favour, beneath this humble roof.

" In the new building, everything will be attentively studied, which can contribute to your easy accommodation ; but, above all, to your perfect safety.

"The avenues and lobbies will be spacious, and the ingress, and egress, to and from every part of the theatre, will be so contrived, that the most desirable facilities will be afforded to the very crowded, brilliant, and overflowing audiences, which the proprietor has the pleasure to anticipate.

"With renewed thanks for past support, and with the hope of future encouragement, in the name of the proprietor, in my own, and in that of all the performers, I heartily, and respectfully, bid you farewell."

Such were the last words addressed to an audience, within the walls of the first Lyceum.

The *débris* of the old theatre having been cleared away, the foundation-stone of the new one was laid, on the 20th of January, 1816, by the wife of the proprietor, who then laid upon it a tablet of copper, engraved with the following inscription :—

ENGLISH OPERA HOUSE.

The first ENGLISH OPERA HOUSE was established
for the encouragement of Native Talent by
SAMUEL JAMES ARNOLD, in the year 1809.
Under the immediate patronage of
HIS MAJESTY KING GEORGE THE THIRD.
And the first stone of this new Theatre was
laid by his Wife, MATILDA CAROLINE ARNOLD,
On the 20th of January, 1816, in the
Fifty-sixth year of his MAJESTY'S reign.

The new theatre, of which Samuel Beazley was the builder, opened on Saturday, the 15th of June, with an occasional address, spoken by Miss Kelly ; the opera of

Up all Night, or the Smuggler's Cave—the piece which had inaugurated Mr. Arnold's management of the former house—and the musical farce of *The Boarding House.* Mr. Bartley, who was now stage-manager, in place of Raymond, apologized, in the course of the evening, for the unfinished state of everything, but as might be expected with such an architect, much taste had been displayed in the fitting-up, and decorations, and the evening, on the whole, passed off extremely well. *The Beggar's Opera, The Castle of Andalusia, The Duenna, The Siege of Belgrade, Artaxerxes, Frederick the Great, Love in a Village, The Maid and the Magpie, One O'Clock,* were successively mounted, but the first season was marked by no new production of any importance. The newly-married Duke and Duchess of Gloucester paid a visit to the new Lyceum, on Friday, the 11th of August; and the Duke and Duchess of Cumberland came on the 17th of the same month. The veteran Incledon sang the part of Macheath, to the Lucy and Polly of Miss Kelly, and Miss Lydia Kelly, on Friday, the 22nd of August, and once more appeared, as Steady, in *The Quaker,* on the 31st. Horn, Isaacs, Wilkinson, Wrench, Bartley, and Miss Kelly, were the leading performers, this season, and that excellent actress, Mrs. Bartley, appeared, for the first and only time, we believe, on these boards, to recite Collins's *Ode to the Passions,* on the last night of the season —the 5th of October. Mrs. Chatterley joined the company in the following year, which was distinguished by nothing else save the introduction of gas, as a means of lighting the house. The English Opera House shared the general depression, which pervaded every class of theatrical property, at this time, and in September the business was so bad, that the device was hit upon, of giving two sets of performances—and, of course, two separate payments for admission—in one evening. The first began at six, and lasted till nine, the second occupying from half-past nine till twelve. These performances were not identical, the earlier one comprising *How to die for Love*, and *Wanted, a Governess;* the other, *Fire and Water*, and *The Woodman's Hut*—a very favourite melodrama. The galleries were very well filled on the first night, but the better classes stayed away, and eventually the smallness of the attendances induced the management to abandon the scheme, at the end of the season—which occurred soon after.

During the next, and for many succeeding winters, the house was occupied—in the intervals between the opera seasons—by Mr. Walker, who gave lectures on Astronomy, entitled *Eidouranion*, and by Mathews, with his inimitable *At Homes*, a mixture of monologue, music, and ventriloquism. Pearman, Harley, and Miss Carew joined the company in 1818, and a still further accession of strength was gained in the celebrated *mime* and character-actor, Mr. T. P. Cooke, for whom the ballet, *La Perouse*, was mounted with much splendour. A new musical farce, *Amateurs and Actors*, by Peake, was produced this season, as well as another, *The Rendezvous*—for Harley, Mr. and Mrs. Chatterley, and Miss Kelly. Both of these proved hits, and remain till now in the recognized repertory of stage-plays. The next year's doings presented nothing remarkable, and it was not until the summer of 1820 that the first real success of the new theatre was obtained. This was with the production—on Wednesday, the 9th of August—of a new "romantic melodrama" by Planché, entitled, *The Vampire, or the Lord of the Isles.* Founding his plot upon Dr. Polidori's tale of Levantine superstition, Mr. Planché transposed the scene to Fingal's Cave, and the Isle of Staffa, which desolate rock— with less regard to local accuracy than stage effect—he endowed with a forest, and a baronial castle. *The Vampire* has always been so completely a tradition of the old Lyceum days, that without transcribing the story, doubtless familiar to every one at all versed in dramatic literature, its original cast should be recorded here.

In the Introductory Vision.

Unda, Spirit of the Flood . ´ .	. Miss Love.
Ariel, Spirit of the Air . . .	. Miss Worgman.
The Vampire	. Mr. T. P. Cooke.
Lady Margaret	. Mrs. Chatterley.

In the Drama.

Ruthven, Earl of Marsden, the Vampire .	Mr. T. P. Cooke.
Ronald, Baron of the Isles . .	. Mr. Bartley.
Robert, his English Attendant .	. Mr. Pearman.
McSwill, the Baron's Henchman .	. Mr. Harley.
Andrew, Steward to Ruthven . .	. Mr. Minton.
Father Francis	. Mr. Shaw.
Lady Margaret, Daughter of Ronald	. Mrs. Chatterley.
Effie, Daughter of Andrew . .	. Miss Carew.
Bridget, Lord Ronald's Housekeeper	. Mrs. Grove.

The thrilling nature of the various situations, the

beauty of the scenery, the charm of the Scotch melodies, and the wonderful conception of the principal character by T. P. Cooke, formed a combination of attractions which could not fail to draw the town, and for some seasons to come this was just one of those things which all playgoers felt they *must* go to see. And although, at this interval, *The Vampire*, in its original form, would probably be found old-fashioned, yet so strong is the leading part, so intense, without being revolting, is the interest, and so ample is the scope for pictorial decoration, that— granting the possession of a Ruthven—we have often thought that it might be advantageously re-fitted for one or other of our modern theatres. Many years after, Mr. Boucicault gave another *Vampire*[2] to the stage, with entirely new scenes and characters, but the incidents proved too realistic—or, in plainer English, too painful —for the general public, and so, despite its merits— which were many—it failed.

In January, 1821, the house was reopened with a miscellaneous entertainment, termed *Soirées Amusantes*, after which Mr. Mathews resumed his *At Homes.* It is a fact worth noticing that Mrs. Glover essayed to play Hamlet, for her benefit, on Monday, the 18th of June, in this year. The season proper commenced soon after with *The Vampire*, to be immediately succeeded by *Rosina, Inkle and Yarico,* and *The Beggar's Opera.* In the latter, Miss Forde, engaged in place of Miss Carew,

[2] At the Princess's Theatre, then under Charles Kean's management, in 1852; and again, in an abridged form, as *The Phantom*, at the Adelphi, in 1862.

appeared as Polly. *The Witch of Derncleugh*, an operatic version of the new and popular novel, "Guy Mannering," was given on the 30th of July, with T. P. Cooke as Dirk Hatteraick, Wilkinson as the Dominie, Pearman, Henry Bertram, and Miss Kelly, Meg Merrilies. John Emery, so noted for his delineation of Yorkshiremen, was next engaged, and on Thursday, the 16th of August, a new melodrama, *The Miller's Maid*, written by Mr. J. F. Savile, and for which Mr. Arnold had composed some music, was produced. The story turned on the love of Giles and George, the miller's men, for his maidservant, Phebe. Bartley played the Miller, Emery, Giles, T. P. Cooke, George, and Miss Kelly, Phebe. The *ensemble* may, therefore, be well imagined. Emery in particular was very fine, and the success of the new play was complete. The season closed on the 27th of September— as it had begun—with *The Vampire*. Mr. Bartley gave a course of Astronomical Lectures in February, 1822. Mr. West—a very old actor—had a benefit on the 7th of April, and on the ensuing night Mr. Granby, from the Dublin Theatre, made his first appearance in London as Sir Edward Mortimer, in *The Iron Chest*. Mr. Granby, later on, long occupied a position of respectability on the metropolitan stage. The celebrated singer, Incledon, took his farewell of the stage on Friday, April the 19th, singing in *The Quaker* and *The Turnpike Gate*. On this occasion Mrs. Glover played Lady Elizabeth Freelove, in *The Day after the Wedding ;* Miss Stephens sang the Echo Song ; and Madame Vestris made her first appearance in a locality where, subsequently, she long reigned supreme, singing, "In infancy our hopes and fears," from the opera of Artaxerxes. The English Opera season began on the 1st of July, with *The Vampire, The Miller's Maid*, and a new operetta, *Love among the Roses*, in which Mr. James Bland made his first appearance in London. The company also included Bartley, Pearman, Wrench, Broadhurst, Wilkinson, Tyrone Power, Henry Phillips, and T. P. Cooke; Misses Kelly, Carew, Carr, Povey, and the juvenile actress, Miss Clara Fisher. Emery was also engaged, but died, almost suddenly,[*] soon after the opening. Miss Clara Fisher attracted some notice in *The Spoiled Child, The Romp*, and similar pieces. A new comic opera, *All in the Dark, or the Banks of the Elbe*, was the first novelty of any importance, and was quite successful. On the 17th of July *Love in a Village* was revived, after a four years' interval, with a rather strong cast, including, Miss Povey as Lucinda, Miss Kelly, Madge, Pearman, Young Meadows, Broadhurst, Eustace, and Bartley, Justice Woodcock. It was heard with much pleasure, and repeated several times. A new melodrama, *Gordon the Gipsy*, with T. P. Cooke and Miss Carr in the leading parts, was brought forward early in August. . In this the very unusual expedient was adopted of leaving the heroine at the end of the play without either lover or husband. *Gordon the Gipsy* succeeded, however, thanks to its well-sustained interest and powerful situations. A new opera in five acts, *Gil Blas at seventeen, twenty-five, and fifty-two*, was next given. Miss Kelly

·³ On the 23rd of July, at the early age of forty-five.

played the part of Gil Blas at seventeen; Pearman, at twenty-five; and Bartley, at fifty-two. To us this would sound "confusion worse confounded," but the opera seems to have had a success which would scarcely be obtained by any play under the same conditions now. On the 31st of August the farce of *Gretna Green* was brought out, in which Miss Kelly's Betty Finnikin remained a tradition to the end of her career, as did also the Jenkins of Wrench. The English opera seems to have been a very profitable speculation this year.

The "events" of 1823 were, the first appearance at the Lyceum of Keeley, who made his entry in a new piece, *The Swing Bridge*—of no particular merit; the engagement of Wallack, who came out as Rhoderick Dhu, in *The Knight of Snowdon*—founded on Scott's *Lady of the Lake*; and the production of a new melodrama, *Presumption, or the Fate of Frankenstein.* The last, notwithstanding its sad and repellent story, remains as another Lyceum memory, owing to the acting of T. P. Cooke as the monster, which at once became the sensation of the season. Mathews also reappeared this summer, playing in the farce of *Monsieur Tonson,* besides giving his popular monologues. There was an unusually good company in 1824. In addition to Bartley, Wrench, Pearman, Broadhurst, Isaacs, Phillips, and Henry Phillips, James Bland, Rayner, Keeley, Power, and T. P. Cooke, Misses Povey, Carr, and Kelly, engagements had been effected with Braham, Mathews, and Miss Stephens, and with the pantomimists, Ellar, Barnes, and J. S. Grimaldi. The elder Grimaldi would also have played for a few nights, had he not been incapacitated by ill-health. The opening opera was *The Barber of Seville*, with "Signor Rossini's celebrated musick," interspersed with gleanings from Dibdin, Phillips, Fioravanti, and Mozart. Fancy the *Barbiere* thus mutilated now ! Yet such usage was very ordinary, in the case of English —and Italian—opera, at the time. Miss Harvey, a *débutante*, as Rosina ; Miss Holdaway, Bertha ; Chapman, Figaro ; Bartley, Bartolo ; J. Isaacs, Basilio ; Broadhurst, Fiorello ; Phillips, Almaviva ; and the afterwards more celebrated Henry Phillips, as Officer of the Guard, were the singers participating in this singular *pasticcio*. It was followed by a new pantomime, *Monkey Island*, in which young Grimaldi, Ellar, Barnes, and Miss Romer appeared. The old burletta *Tom Thumb* was next revived with Master Burke as the hero ; and Braham returned, to sing Count Belino, in *The Devil's Bridge*. The foot of the play-bills, from the commencement of the season, had contained a paragraph to the effect that "a New Musical Performance of an extraordinary character" was in active preparation. This statement was explained, and the mystery solved, on Thursday, the 22nd of July—a night ever memorable in the annals of the Lyceum—by the production, for the first time in England, of the celebrated Weber's equally celebrated opera *Der Freyschütz*, here described as "an eccentric vehicle for musick, and scenick effect," and of which we subjoin the cast :—

Ottocar	. . . . .	Mr. Baker.
Kuno .	. . . .	Mr. Bartley.

Rudolph . . . . . Mr. Braham.
Caspar . . . . . Mr. Bennett.
Rollo . . . . . Mr. Henry Phillips.
Killian . . . . . Mr. Tayleure.
Agnes . . . . . Miss Noel.
Ann . . . . . Miss Povey.
Witch of the Wolf's Glen . . Mrs. Bryan.

The Bridesmaids were represented by Mrs. Weippert, Miss Holdaway, and other ladies of the company. Miss Romer led the waltz, in the first act, and the chorus and orchestra were augmented for the occasion. The characters were, one and all, most carefully rendered, Braham in particular being considered to have surpassed himself, both in singing and acting, as Rudolph, whilst as for the Zamiel of Mr. T. P. Cooke, well might the critic of a daily paper—the *Morning Post*—describe this actor as being endowed with " that peculiar talent, which is sure to place every devil, vampire, spirit, or nondescript, in his own especial keeping." It was agreed, on all sides, that nothing in its way so startling, or so powerful, had ever been seen before. The success of *Der Freyschütz* was literally unbounded. London seemed suddenly to have gone wild upon the subject. Its music was to be heard in every drawing-room, and the opera, in one form or another, was speedily attempted at nearly every theatre throughout the kingdom. As a matter of course also, the two Patent Houses had elaborately mounted versions prepared for their ensuing winter campaigns. But from all and each—in right perhaps of its Zamiel—the English Opera House was held to have borne away the palm, and to this very day, old playgoers invariably associate *Der Freyschütz* with the Lyceum—whilst they rarely refer to the Lyceum, without reverting to the glories of *Der Freyschütz.*

Subsequently Miss Stephens, and Miss Paton, in turn replaced Miss Noel as Agnes, in *Der Freyschütz*, which ran with scarcely an interruption, up to the end of the season. Early in the next one, a Miss Goward made her first appearance in London, as Rosina, in Shield's ballad opera of that name, and, on the same evening, as Little Pickle, in *The Spoiled Child.* Miss Goward was even then credited by the Press with a voice, and musical cultivation, of no mean excellence, as well as with considerable comic powers, gifts—especially the last—which, in years to come, were found developed in such rare perfection, in Mrs. Keeley. For the rest, the Lyceum rested chiefly on its former triumphs, the novelties produced being all inferior, with the exception of a little piece *The Shepherd's Boy*, in which a scene of recognition, between Cooper, as the Marquis de la Tour, and Miss Kelly, as Alexis, was acted by both in their finest manner, and created a profound impression. A new act-drop had been painted for the theatre, by the scenic artists, Thomas and William Grieve, previous to the season of 1826. The tenor Sapio replaced Braham, this year, appearing, in conjunction with Miss Paton, and Henry Phillips—now advanced to a leading position—in *Tarrare*, an ineffective opera by Salieri, which had been brought out the year before. The prevailing taste for the supernatural was amply gratified this summer, by the production of *The Death-Fetch, or the Student of Gottingen.* This was founded on the Irish story of The Fetches, in "Tales of the O'Hara Family," and the scene changed to Germany. The music was composed and arranged by Mr. C. Horn. Admirably got up, and very well acted and sung by Archer, Bartley, Pearman, Keeley, and the Misses Paton, Goward, and Kelly, *The Death-Fetch* had a success which placed it in the stock-repertory of the house, and it may still be met with occasionally, we believe, in the provinces. Winter's opera, *The Oracle*, produced in its integrity in August, expensively mounted, and aided by the exertions of Thorne, Sapio, Miss Paton, and Miss Goward, was also most favourably received. The first event of 1827, was the revival, on the opening night, the 2nd of July, of Dryden's *masque, Arthur and Emmeline.* The music, selected from the compositions of Purcell, was sung by Pearman, Thorne, Henry Phillips, Miss Paton, and Miss Kelly. It was followed by a new melodrama *The Cornish Miners*, with incidental music by George Herbert Rodwell. O'Smith made his *début* in this piece, as successor to the line of characters previously played by T. P. Cooke. On the 20th of July, Miss Betts, afterwards so long associated with Drury Lane, under Mr. Bunn, made her first appearance on any stage, as Rosetta, in *Love in a Village.* On the 24th, *The Serjeant's Wife*, a drama in two acts, by John Banim, was given, in which Miss Kelly as Lisette, and Miss Goward as Margot, quite transcended themselves. Bartley, Pearman, Keeley, James Bland, and O'Smith were also cast for this play, the absorbing interest of which carried it through the season, and obviated the necessity of any further novelty, although *The Freebooters*, by Paër—best remembered as the composer of *Agnese*—was also mounted, in August, with Miss Betts, in the part of Isabella.

. Mathews, and his *At Homes*, were displaced in the spring of 1828, by the French company, who had previously played at the more distant theatre in Tottenham Street. They opened with Molière's *Tartuffe*, and remained at the Lyceum, which had been most gorgeously redecorated for their reception, till the middle of June. The principal performers were Perlet, Laurent, Laporte, Préval, Mademoiselles Irma, Falcon, and Jenny Vertpré. The English Opera season began on Monday, the 30th of June, when Miss Harriet Cawse sang in *The Freebooters*. On the next night, Madame Féron came out as Rosina, in *The Barber of Seville*. On this occasion *The Vampire* was the after-piece, and served to introduce Mr. James Vining —from Bath—to a London audience, as Ruthven. On Monday, the 7th of July, *The Bottle Imp*, a new melodrama, by R. B. Peake, with music by G. H. Rodwell, was brought out, with O'Smith as the Imp, James Vining, Keeley, Wood, and the Misses Cawse, in the other parts. The story of *The Bottle Imp* was based upon the German legend, that the possessor of a bottle imp could command riches, power, and prosperity of every kind, at the mere wish, but that if he retained the spirit to the end of his life, his soul was forfeited to the Evil One. Meanwhile he had the privilege of disposing of the bottle, provided he sold it for less than he gave. The adventures of this bottle made up a most exciting and interesting play, the success of which was decided. *The Noyades, or Love and Gratitude*, was the next novelty. This was a well-written little two-act piece, relating to the French Revolution, in which Miss Kelly made a great effect. It was followed by the musical farce *He Lies like Truth*, with a good part for Wrench. On the 27th of July was given an English version of Mozart's *Così fan Tutti*, entitled *Tit for Tat*, with Madame Féron as Despina, Miss Betts and Miss Cawse as the sisters Fiordelisa and Dorabella, and Henry Phillips—carrying away all the honours—as Alfonso. The opera, got up under Mr. Hawes's superintendence, was warmly applauded. *Not for me, or the New Apple of Discord*, being another version of *'Twas I*, was the next novelty, on the 23rd of August. Weigl's *Gli Amori Marinari* was next adapted to the English stage, as *The Pirate of Genoa*. It was produced early in September, with H. Phillips, and Madame Féron, when the light and agreeable character of the music, and its excellent rendering, gained for the opera a success. An operetta, *The Quartette, or Interrupted Harmony*, given on the 18th of September, was the last event of a very enterprising and remunerative season.

Some alterations in the gas-fittings necessitating the temporary close of Covent Garden Theatre, the company came over to the English Opera House, for a brief series of performances during the winter. On the first of these, Edmund Kean played Richard III., to the Richmond of Charles Kemble, and the Lady Anne of Miss Jarman—afterwards Mrs. Ternan. Miss Jarman next played Rosalind, in *As You Like It*, to the Orlando of Charles Kemble.

L

Kean also played Shylock, in *The Merchant of Venice*, with Charles Kemble as Bassanio, Miss Jarman as Portia, and Miss Goward, Nerissa. In *The Belle's Stratagem*, Charles Kemble was Doricourt, and the comedian Green, —best known in the green-room as "Gentleman" Green—Flutter. Kean, also played Sir Giles Overreach, in *A New Way to Pay Old Debts*, to the Wellborn of C. Kemble. The latter, and Miss Jarman appeared as Mr. and Mrs. Oakley, in *The Jealous Wife*. Kean played Othello, to the Iago of Warde, and the Cassio of Charles Kemble; and the same eminent tragedian also appeared as Sir Edward Mortimer in *The Iron Chest*. Lastly, Madame Vestris took the part of Mrs. Page, with Bartley as Falstaff, in *The Merry Wives of Windsor*. Madame Vestris also appeared in the after-piece of *The Invincibles*. These performances lasted from Monday, the 17th of November, to Monday, the 1st of December, and certainly form an interesting addition to the chronicles of the theatre. The French company returned in January, 1829. Lafont, and Mademoiselle Jenny Coulon were added to the *troupe*, which remained here till the beginning of June, and on the 27th of that month the house reopened for the English Opera season. The company now comprised Sapio, Henry Phillips, Wood, Bartley, James Bland, James Vining, Keeley, O'Smith, Miss Kelly, Miss Goward—who had lately changed her name, and become Mrs. Keeley— Miss Betts, the Misses Cawse, ˙Miss Pincott—now Mrs. Alfred Wigan—and the excellent actress of old women, Mrs. C. Jones. To these may be added Mr. Frank

Matthews, who made his first appearance, on the 1st of July, as Waldeck, in *The Bottle Imp*. The direction of the music was again confided to Mr. Hawes. The first novelty was a romantic drama, *The Sister of Charity*, which had a marked success, owing to the fine acting of Miss Kelly, as Sister Ursula. *The Robber's Bride*, an opera from the German, composed by Ferdinand Ries, was produced, on the 15th of July, with Sapio, Henry Phillips, and Miss Betts. A three-act piece by Peake, with music by Rodwell, *The Spring Lock*, was also given with success, on the 18th of August. The most important event of the season, however, was the production, on the 25th of that month, of Marschner's opera *Der Vampyr*. The libretto, the story of which was identical with that of his pretty melodrama, was translated by Planché, but in the opera the scene was laid—as in the original tale—in the Banat of Lemiswar. Henry Phillips was the Vampire, Count Mavrocordato, and acquitted himself admirably in a most difficult part. The success of *Der Vampyr* was decided, though it did not create anything like the enthusiasm aroused by Der Freyschütz. The house closed on Friday, the 2nd of October, and it may be interesting to note that the last performance consisted of *The Spring Lock*, *Sold for a Song*, and *The Bottle Imp*. The French company, reinforced by Portier, and Mademoiselle St. Ange, came back at the beginning of the new year. But their prospects, which were more than usually hopeful, were quickly blighted by the total destruction of the second Lyceum, by fire, early in the morning of Thursday, the 16th of February 1830.

The cause of this disaster was never directly brought home, but might probably have been traced to a defect in the gas pipes. There had been a performance on the night before, and the smell of escaping gas was then very perceptible. Whatever the reason, the result was doubly unfortunate, for the public thus lost a beautiful and favourite resort, whilst the proprietor, being entirely uninsured, was left, as it seemed, an all but ruined man. But Mr. Arnold was not the man to sit down beneath misfortune. Keeping together the *personnel* of his theatre, he carried on the English Opera, for the next three or four seasons, at the Adelphi, or Olympic, devising in the meantime plans for the restoration of his own house. The inability of raising money, for some time rendered this impracticable, but all obstacles having been at length removed, the Lyceum was again rebuilt, and opened—once more under the familiar title of the English Opera House—on Monday, the 14th of July, 1834. The architect, as before, was Samuel Beazley, who had made considerable alterations in the external structure, placing the principal entrance in Wellington Street, the old one, towards the Strand, being now set apart for the frequenters of the pit only. The audience part of the new building was, at the time, considered—as in our opinion it still remains —by far the handsomest, and best-proportioned, of all the London theatres. Mr. Hawes was reappointed director of the music, and a new post, that of melo-dramatic director, was assigned to the popular actor O'Smith. Serle succeeded Bartley, in the management of the stage. The inaugural performance consisted of *The Yeoman's*

Daughter, Call again To-morrow, and a former Lyceum success, *Amateurs and Actors*. Mr. Serle spoke a rhymed address, and amongst the old favourites were recognized Mr. and Mrs. Keeley, Wrench, Frank Matthews, Oxberry, John Reeve, James Bland, and Miss Pincott, together with Wilson, Henry Phillips, and Mrs. Waylett. Miss Romer should also be added. The first novelty of any importance, in the new theatre, was an opera, *Nourjahad*, the maiden essay of a young composer, Mr. Edward Loder, son of John Loder, and pupil of Ferdinand Ries. The book was written by Mr. Arnold. The opera had an encouraging reception, and some portions of it were much admired, particularly a trio, "Soft is the murmur," and a barytone song, "There's a light in her laughing eye." The singers were Wilson, H. Phillips, Misses Healey and Romer. Unfortunately, *Nourjahad* did nothing for the treasury, but another new opera, brought out a few weeks later, had a much more substantial result. This was *The Mountain Sylph*, set by John Barnett to a story nearly identical with that of the ballet, *La Sylphide*—inseparably linked with the famous name of Taglioni. In the opera, Miss Romer was the Sylph ; Wilson, Donald ; Keeley, Christie ; and Henry Phillips, the Wizard, Hela. The success of *The Mountain Sylph*, at the time, was really *immense*, and although, as an opera, it has long since most undeservedly passed out of hearing, yet the air, "Farewell to the mountain," and the trio, "This magic-wove scarf," will never be forgotten, so long as a feeling and love for melody remain. *The Mountain Sylph* ran with boundless applause, to overflowing houses, for fifty-eight consecutive nights, an almost unprecedented occurrence, so far as an opera was concerned, in those days. Among the lesser events of the season, which ended in the middle of November, were, the production of a little drama, *Cramond Brig*—still an accepted after-piece—with some introduced Scotch airs, delightfully warbled by Wilson ; and an operetta, *Geneviève*, adapted from the French, by Mrs. Cornwall Baron Wilson, and the music of which unpretending trifle was written by Mr. G. A. Macfarren. A spectral drama, *The Death Guest*, though much belauded in the bills, failed to command anything of a run.

The year 1835 was ushered in by a series of French plays, with Frederick Lemaitre and Jenny Vertpré. The former made quite a sensation in *Robert Macaire* and *Trente Ans, ou La Vie d'un Joueur*. Mr. Arnold re-opened his house at Easter with a new opera, written by Miss Mitford, and composed by Mr. Packer, entitled *Sadak and Kalasrade, or the Waters of Oblivion*, into which, by the way, it was speedily submerged, so undramatic alike were the music and the tale. A new farce, *My Fellow Clerk*, by John Oxenford, in which Miss P. Horton and Mrs. Frank Matthews made their first appearance here, and a new drama, *The Shadow on the Wall*, by T. J. Serle, which followed, were unequivocally successful. Mrs. Keeley's acting in the last was found quite equal to that of Miss Kelly in her best days. An English version of *La Sonnambula*, for Miss Romer, was next given, and another farce by Oxenford, *I and My Double ;* and a little later an opera by Mr. Rodwell, *The*

Spirit of the Bell, the music of which, if unambitious, was unaffectedly pleasing. Ices were distributed, gratis, to the occupants of the pit and boxes during the hot weather which prevailed in June and July, and the manager issued an odd advertisement, to the effect that " in consequence of its complete ventilation, the temperature of this theatre is many degrees cooler than that of the external atmosphere." Neither ices nor the promise of a cool temperature, unfortunately, sufficed to allure the public into a theatre which, since its rebuilding, they seemed somehow to have taken far less kindly to, than in the old days ; and finally, owing to his heavy pecuniary losses, Mr. Arnold, whose many years of managerial enterprise and activity certainly merited a very different fate—was compelled to withdraw from the direction at the end of July.

Some of the company now formed themselves into a commonwealth, and reopened the house on the 10th of August with a new Scotch drama, *The Covenanters*, in which a Mr. McIan made a strong impression by his admirable acting. The incidental music was selected, and partly composed, by Mr. Edward Loder. Another drama, *The Old Oak Tree*, with music by Macfarren, was also received with favour. An English version of Mercadanti's *Elisa e Claudio* was given early in September, with no result except the introduction of the bass singer, Mr. Stretton, to a London audience. A new romantic drama, *The Dice of Death*, with O'Smith as Mephistopheles, and for which Loder had composed some pretty music, was produced in the middle of September. Mr.

Rayner, after many years' absence, returned to the
Lyceum, as Giles, in *The Miller's Maid*, in October.   In
November, a new drama, by Bayle Bernard, *Woman's
Faith*, proved to be an extremely good and successful play.
Mr. Denvil made his first appearance here at Christmas, in
a piece called *Minerali*, and a pantomime, *Ride a Cock-
Horse*, was got up, of which the chief merit lay in its
clown, Harry Boleno.   The house closed early in 1836,
but was opened with concerts in March, in which Clara
Novello, Madame Caradori-Allan, and Mrs. Alfred Shaw
took part, and on the 21st of this month Sheridan Knowles
played Julian St. Pierre, in his own drama, *The Wife of
Mantua*, for a benefit.   On Easter Monday, the English
Opera House was again opened by a commonwealth, who
engaged a good company, with Mr. J. H. Tully as
musical director.   Their opening novelty was a drama by
Bayle Bernard, *Lucille, a Tale of the Heart*, which, with
Mrs. Keeley, Miss P. Horton, Williams, and Oxberry, in
the leading characters, deservedly made a great hit.   The
plot of this drama was founded upon a story in Bulwer's
" Pilgrims of the Rhine." Mrs. Nisbett and Miss Jane
Mordaunt next appeared in *The Captain's Not a Miss.*
Meyerbeer's *Les Huguenots*, arranged by Mr. Tully, as—
will it be believed ?—a " Grand Musical Drama in Two
Acts," with Mrs. Keeley as Valentine, was mounted on
the 25th of April.   The best comment on this unfortunate
production will be to give the duration of its run—three
nights !   Miss Murray, a charming actress, whose career
was prematurely cut short by death, was added to the
company in May, in a new piece by Oxenford, *The Gun-*

powder Plot. On Monday, the 13th of June, a new domestic drama, in three acts, by Bayle Bernard, entitled
The Farmer's Story, with Mrs. Keeley—who seems to
have been, at this time, the prop of the house—as Mary
Lockwood, was produced, and achieved a marked and
thoroughly deserved success. Mrs. Fitzwilliam played in
July, and in August the American comedian, Mr. Hackett,
drew the town, as Wildfire, in *The Kentuckian.* Mr.
Leffler came out in September, as Hela, in *The Mountain
Sylph*, in which Wilson and Miss Shirreff also sang. A
new operatic drama, founded on Byron's " Corsair," *The
Pacha's Bridal*, written by Mark Lemon, and for which
a young composer, Mr. Frederick Romer, supplied some
very pleasing music, was, in addition, presented about the
same time. Yates gave his *Imitations*, for Miss Betts'
benefit, on the 3rd of November, and Madame Vestris and
Charles Mathews played in *The Loan of a Lover*, for
Peake's (the treasurer) benefit, on the 15th of the same
month, which was also the last night of the season.

The well-known librarian, Mr. Mitchell, of Bond Street,
with the active co-operation of Signor and Madame
Puzzi,[4] engaged the Lyceum for a season of Italian Opera

* The celebrated horn-player, Giovanni Puzzi, was born at
Parma in 1793, and was educated at Fontanellato, in that
duchy. Giving evidence, from his earliest years, of a great
musical talent, he was sent, at the age of fourteen, to Paris
by an Italian nobleman, Count Sanvitali, whose two sons had
been his schoolfellows. Immediately on his arrival in Paris
he was introduced to the composer Paër, who, after hearing
him play, at once procured him an engagement in the private
band of the Emperor Napoleon, and also as principal soloist

Buffa, this winter. The operas given were *L'Elisir d'Amore, Il Furioso* (Donizetti), *Scaramuccia, La Chiara*

in the orchestra of the *Théâtre Italien.* A few years later, in 1814, on the recommendation of the great Duke of Wellington, he removed to London, where he eventually settled for life. Through the patronage of the Duke he speedily obtained an excellent position in the artistic world, and the direction of nearly all private concerts, as well as those of the court of King George IV. The personal friend of three successive managers of the Opera-house in the Haymarket— Ebers, Laporte, and Lumley—he was during a long series of years selected to negotiate the engagements for the opera, a post for which he was particularly fitted, owing to his remarkable tact and address, combined, moreover, as these qualities were, with a thorough knowledge of business. Camporese, Catalani, Colbran-Rossini (wife of the great composer), Signor and Madame Ronzi di Begnis, Pasta, Pisaroni, David, Donzelli, Rubini, Persiani, Grisi, Mario, Coletti, Frezzolini, Tadolini, Barbieri-Nini, and many others, were all introduced to England through the instrumentality of Signor Puzzi, and the last acquisitions due to his good offices were the still remembered favourites, Marietta Piccolomini and Antonio Giuglini. Amongst those whom he sent over in 1827 was the Signora Giacinta Toso, whom he described in a letter to Ebers as *belle comme une ange, jeune de dix-neuf ans, élève du Conservatoire de Milan.* The attractions, both of voice and person, of Mademoiselle Toso, were found on her arrival to fully justify this description, but within a very few months she became the wife of Puzzi, and a little later retired from the stage. Both Signor and Madame Puzzi, however, continued their connexion with the King's—known later as Her Majesty's—Theatre, as the friendly negotiators of engagements with the artists, combining this with the private teaching of music and singing, but their connexion with the Opera ceased soon after the retirement of Mr.

di Rosenberg (Ricci), *Nina Pazza* (Coppola), *Un Anno ed un Giorno* (Benedict), and *Le Nozze de Figaro* (Mozart), sung by Mademoiselle Blasis, Miss Fanny Wyndham, and Mademoiselle Giannoni, Signori Torri, Catone, Ruggiero, Bellini, and Sebastiano Ronconi. There was a good orchestra, selected from that of the King's Theatre, with Mori as leader and Benedict as conductor. Blasis and Torri were already known as artists of experience, Miss Fanny Wyndham, afterwards Madame F. Lablache, made a most successful *début*, and the beautiful Mademoiselle Giannoni,[*] as the demented heroine of Coppola's opera, then showed an almost exceptional promise, but seems never to have been heard of after this season. Sebastiano Ronconi was an excellent buffo, and the lovely tenor of Signor Catone charmed every hearer. All the operas pleased, and especially *Le Nozze*, which was a brilliant success. The *Chiara di Rosenberg* was interesting, as serving to disprove the malicious statement previously circulated to the effect that Balfe had appropriated the music

Lumley. Signor Puzzi died a few years since, but his widow, in conjunction with two of her daughters, both very clever musicians, still continues to give lessons in singing. Few members of the musical profession at any time, have been more respected in public, or more beloved in private life, than the entire Puzzi family.

[*] Chorley, in his *Thirty Years' Musical Reminiscences*, vol. ii. page 5, has accidentally confounded Mademoiselle Giannoni with Madame Ronconi—wife of the famous barytone, Giorgio Ronconi—who sang with little success at Her Majesty's Theatre in 1842, and at Covent Garden in 1847. The two singers, however, were not identical. They were sisters.

for his own *Siege of Rochelle*.   The two works were now
found to be totally dissimilar, and as a matter of fact, Balfe's
was much the best opera of the two.   Lafont, Monsieur
and Madame Allen, and Mademoiselle Vertpré then gave
a series of French performances, and in July Mr. Bunn
took the reins, opening on the 24th of that month with
Balfe's *Catherine Grey*, sung by the composer, Seguin,
S. Jones, Misses Rainforth and Romer.   That favourite
and admirable actor, Compton, made his entry on the
London boards on the same night, as Robin, in the
ballad opera of *The Waterman*. The celebrated Pasta sang
" Di tanti palpiti," on the stage of the Lyceum, for the
benefit of M. Bernard on Friday, the 28th of July, 1837.
A new melodrama, *Blanche of Jersey*, written by Peake,
with music by John Barnett, had a genuine success in
August.   Amongst other events we find the old burletta
Midas, revived about this time, with Apollo, Miss Romer ;
Daphne, Miss Rainforth ; Mysis, Mrs. C. Jones ; Nysa,
Miss Poole, and Midas, Mr. Williams.   Mr. Bunn's
tenancy expired at Michaelmas.   Mr. Mitchell began a
second season of Opera Buffa on the 16th of November,
with Mesdames Franceschini, Scheroni, Bellini, Miss
Fanny Wyndham, and Madame Eckerlin, Signori Catone,
Sanquirico, Bellini, Castellan, and Frederico Lablache.
As before, M. Benedict was the conductor.   The operas
given were *L'Italiana in Algieri, L'Inganno Felice* (Rossini), *L'Elisir d'Amore, Betly* (Donizetti) *Scaramuccia,
Il Nuovo Figaro* (Ricci), *Elisa e Claudio* (Mercadante),
Nina Pazza (Coppola), and *Le Nozze de Figaro* (Mozart).
Miss Wyndham had improved greatly, the *début* of young

Lablache was interesting, and Catone's sympathetic organ was more admired than ever, but as a whole the company proved inferior to last year's, Madame Eckerlin, upon whose shoulders the burden of prima-donnaship principally rested, being an artist with a fine method, but an almost extinguished voice.

The English Opera House was again managed by a commonwealth in the summer of 1838. *The Queen's Command*, " a Dramatic Sketch in Four Scenes," introduced—on the 14th of July—a Mr. William Shakespeare, as the poet. The " sketch " and the actor were both failures. The real name of the latter, it is said, was Walton. On Monday, the 13th of August, a new opera by G. A. Macfarren, *The Devil's Opera*, was produced. The libretto, written by the composer's father, was meant as a satire upon the taste for *diablerie* prevalent at the time, and which had resulted in such opera-books as *Der Freyschütz*, *Robert le Diable*, and others. The story bore upon a plot entered into by the friends of a certain Marchese Posilipo, to cure him of his love of the study of necromancy, by passing off a black slave, named Diavoletto, as the real Devil. Hence the title *The Devil's Opera*. This was the first work of pretention emanating from the pen of the then very young composer. The chief fault brought against it by the critics was that Mr. Macfarren had treated in too serious a style a libretto which was obviously a mere satire. The music nevertheless had much merit, and the concerted pieces were most skilfully treated. Of these, a trio " Good Night," sung by Miss Rainforth, Miss Poole, and Mrs. Seguin, was considered the gem. The other singers were Messrs. Frazer,

Seguin, and S. Jones. Miss Poole, at that time very young, disguised herself as an old *gouvernante*, very cleverly. Wieland's pantomime, as the mysterious slave, and would-be demon, Diavoletto, was something marvellous. He was universally acknowledged as the finest *mime* seen since Grimaldi, and a worthy representative of the great school of Dubois. *The Devil's Opera* was completely successful. About this time a benefit was got up for the once celebrated pantaloon, Barnes, whose circumstances were greatly reduced by the ill-health which for some time had prevented him from following his profession. Besides the company who were singing in *The Devil's Opera*, Cooper, Leffler, Ducrow, and Mrs. Fitzwilliam gave their services, and Wieland devised a pantomime scene, *Shakespeare's Seven Ages*, in which Barnes did "the lean and slippered pantaloon,". supported by several pantomimists, the principal of whom being Hartland, Ellar, Montgomery, and Miss Fairbrother. The following pathetic address was also written for the occasion, and delivered by its author Leman Rede :—

> "Who has not felt, as time and care creep on,
> And childhood's laughing hours are faded, gone,
> Memory turn back with fond and lingering gaze,
> To Christmas revels and to boyhood's days ?
> Cast back your thoughts to twenty years ago—
> (I don't expect the ladies can do so)—
> Have you no visions of a Parker's grace ?
> Bologna's elegance ? Grimaldi's face ?
> And 'mid that merry throng, in life's gay noon,
> Of Barnes, the lean and slipper'd Pantaloon ? .
> Ye knew him *then ;* and by each radiant brow
> That smiles around me, he's remember'd now.

Your presence proves *your* memory, and *his* worth.
And you, the fairest portion of the earth,
And younger spirits, hearing in his name
But the faint echo of a bygone fame,
Gazed ye with joy upon the sable sprite
Who won your laughter and applause to-night?
Think as you linger on that fairy scene
What Wieland is, poor Barnes may once have been.
Turn, and behold that creature lying low,
A pining sufferer, in want, in woe ;
Shall he, who made your childhood's laughter, live
Needing the succour that your hands can give?
Or ye young hearts, which no such memories haunt,
Though ye know not his merits, feel his want ;
Together cheer the couch of age and pain,
And bid the grief-chill'd mourner smile again.
Or, oh ! if tears must yet that cheek bedew,
Let them—they're tears of gratitude to you.
You are not feebly thank'd by him alone,
For his heart's joy is echo'd by your own.
The charity by which that lorn one lives
Blesses alike both him who takes and gives.
His heartfelt prayer he offers up to you,
Props of his age, Heaven bless you, and adieu ! "

Poor Barnes only survived till the 28th of this month.
Mr. Elton appeared in *Rob Roy* on the 6th of September.
The season closed with the thirty-sixth representation of
The Devil's Opera, on Friday, the 28th of September.

A Signor Negri conducted some Promenade Concerts,
at Christmas, and early in 1839; and on Easter Monday
Mr. Penley tried his hand at management, with a good
company, including Mrs. Stirling, Messrs. Creswick,
Addison, Henry Bedford, and the comedian Vale. Mr.
Penley's management unfortunately collapsed in a very

short time, but the house seems to have been occasionally
opened for benefits, in May and June, and at one of
these Mrs. Honey appeared, in *The Married Rake.* On
Monday, the 22nd of July, the composer Balfe—in those
days also, a barytone singer of no mean reputation—
opened here, playing Count Zeno, in his own opera,
Diadeste. Frazer, Leffler, and Miss Rainforth made up
the operatic *corps.* Balfe's brief season, which lasted till
the 31st of August, was marked by one or two other incidents worthy of commemoration. The pantomimist, Norman, the friend and contemporary of Grimaldi, played in
the melodrama, *Frankenstein,* revived as an after-piece ;
Grisi, Persiani, Tamburini, and Rubini, sung in a concert,
on Monday, the 17th of August, for the benefit of a
fellow artist, Signor di Angioli ; and *La Sonnambula* was
given, on the last night of the season, for the manager's
benefit, when Madame Balfe—formerly Mademoiselle Lina
Roser—made her first appearance on the English stage, as
Amina, with very distinguished success. Balfe now
withdrew, but the Lyceum was kept going for another
month, by some members of the company, who played
in a new ballad opera, *The Lass of Gowrie,* and in the
old melodrama, *The Miller and His Men.* Mr. Morris
Barnett also appeared in *Monsieur Jacques,* and the clown,
Tom Matthews, in his great master Grimaldi's pantomime
Puck and the Puddings. The house then reverted, for
several months, to Promenade Concerts, but theatrical
performances were again given in the summer of 1840,
by a portion of the Covent Garden company, consisting
of Mrs. Orger, Mrs. Walter Lacy—a most pleasing and

accomplished actress, who retired far too soon from professional life, Mrs. Brougham, Miss Cooper, Messrs. T. Green, Brougham, Compton, George Wild, and Granby. Mrs. Walter Lacy delivered an address on the opening night, written by Mark Lemon, and sustained the leading part in a new drama, *The Three Secrets*, from the same hand. Mr. W. S. Emden was the stage-manager of this venture, and Miss Kelly returned for one night to the scene of so many bygone triumphs, to play Lucy Lockit, in *The Beggar's Opera*, for Frank Matthews' benefit, on Monday, the 31st of August.

In March, 1841, Balfe once more took the Lyceum, for the production of his opera, *Keolanthe*, which in spite of its not very happily-chosen libretto—by Mr. E. Fitz-Ball—charmed every one, by the freshness, elegance, and thorough melodiousness of its music. In the part of Keolanthe, Madame Balfe proved herself to be, both in singing, and acting, a complete artist of the good old school; Miss Gould, a pupil of John Barnett, made a very promising *début*; and the other parts were most creditably filled by Wilson, H. Phillips, and Stretton. The composer himself conducted an excellent orchestra, on the occasion. On Tuesday, the 30th of March, the Queen paid her first visit to the Lyceum, for the purpose of hearing *Keolanthe*. The experiment, however, in a financial sense, unfortunately did not answer, and after a season much less prosperous than it deserved to be, the house closed, on Saturday, the 15th of May. The drama was again attempted during the summer months, Mrs. Glover, Mrs. Waylett, Miss Fortescue, Mrs.

M

Selby, and Mr. T. P. Cooke being the principal exponents, and at the end of August, "The Council of Dramatic Authors" leased the theatre, for the production of a drama, *Martinucci*, written by Mr. George Stephens, which was rendered interesting as introducing Mr. Phelps, and Mrs. Warner, to a Lyceum audience. This was the only occasion, we believe, on which these artists ever played there. Elton also had a part in this play, which although not well received by the critics, had a short run. Jullien, and his band, were here early in 1842, and a few months later, on the break-up of the Vestris management, at Covent Garden, the principal members of that company opened at the Lyceum. The company was a very good one, including, as it did, the names of Harley, J. Bland, Walter Lacy, J. Vining, Brougham, Frank Matthews, Oxberry, and Alfred Wigan, Mesdames Brougham, Humby, Jane Mordaunt, Murray, Pincott, Marshall, and the dancer, Miss Ballin. The house existed chiefly on revivals, but a new burletta, *The Water Witches*, was produced, on the 6th of June. Carter exhibited his lions in September, and on the 28th of that month, Pierce Egan played Bob Logic, in a version of *Tom and Jerry*, now entitled *Life in Dublin*, for his benefit. Jullien gave another series of concerts in December, and Van Amburgh opened the house as a circus, at the beginning of 1843. Mrs. Waylett—so renowned for her exquisite ballad-singing—was manageress at Easter, in this year, when Mr. Samuel Emery—son of John Emery—made his first appearance in London, choosing for his *début* his father's great part of Giles, in *The Miller's Maid.* Mrs. Waylett gave up the management at the end of May, and the house then remained closed for several months. Jullien next re-occupied it, in the middle of November, giving his concerts up to Christmas. On the 29th of January, in the following year, Captain Harvey Tuckett, whose *physique* enabled him to dispense with padding, essayed to play Falstaff, in *The Merry Wives of Windsor*, but like everything else at this unfortunate theatre, the attempt ended in failure, and within a fortnight it closed again.

Fortune nevertheless at length deigned to smile upon the long luckless Lyceum, when—on Easter Monday, the 8th of April, 1844—it was opened, under the lessee-ship and management of Mr. and Mrs. Keeley. It is a fact, we believe, very little known, that towards the close of 1843, an agreement had been all but signed, constituting Phelps, Anderson, and Keeley, the joint lessees of the Lyceum, for the performance of the Poetic Drama. At the last moment, however, the affair " went off," and eventually Keeley entered upon the direction alone. It is interesting to reflect upon " what might have been," had the original plan been carried out, though the chances are, in our opinion, that such a combination could not have had any long continuance. With three such luminaries sitting in conjunction upon the managerial throne, a conflict of interests must soon have arisen, and then one or other would have gone to some other theatre. And what the Keeleys [*] thought of *their* fitness

---

[*] And yet there were few finer exponents of the comic characters of the Shakspearian drama—as, for instance,

for the Poetic Drama, was doubtless expressed in the following lines of the inaugural address, written by Gilbert A'Beckett, and delivered with all her accustomed point by Mrs. Keeley:—

> "The drama called legitimate may thrive
> As well in two or three acts as in five.
> Man by his mind, not by his height, we rate;
> Talent, not length, makes plays legitimate."

Burlesque was the class of entertainment upon which the new management mainly relied, and that on the opening-night, on the subject of the *Forty Thieves*—by Gilbert A'Beckett and Mark Lemon—with Miss Fairbrother as an extremely attractive Abdallah, at once hit the taste of the public. *Open Sesame* was followed, at intervals by *Aladdin* (Albert Smith and Charles Kenney), *Whittington and his Cat, Cinderella, The Enchanted Horse* (all by Albert Smith and Tom Taylor); *Hop o' my Thumb* (Albert Smith)—to introduce the American dwarf, Tom Thumb, in March, 1846; *Robin Hood, The Magic Horn, The Enchanted Forest* (Charles Dance), and *The Wood Demon, or One o'Clock* (Albert Smith and Charles Kenney). A series of adaptations of Charles Dickens' novels were also brought out, the first being a version of *Martin Chuzzlewit*—with Keeley as Mrs. Gamp—by Mr. Edward Stirling, with a prologue by Albert Smith, which we append:—

> "We owe this story of the present hour
> . To that great master-hand whose graphic power

Touchstone and Audrey, or Launcelot Gobbo and Nerissa— than this exceptionally gifted pair.

Can call up laughter, bid the tear to start,
And find an echoing chord in every heart ;
Whom we have learn'd to deem a household friend ;
Who midst his varied writings never penn'd
One line that might his guileless pages spot,
One word that dying he would wish to blot."

The Chimes, by Mr. E. Stirling, at Christmas, 1844, and *The Cricket on the Hearth,* by Albert Smith, in December, 1845, with S. Emery as John Peerybingle ; Keeley, Caleb Plummer ; Miss Louisa Howard, May Fielding ; Miss Mary Keeley, Bertha ; Miss Turner, Tilly Slowboy ; and Mrs. Keeley (who was never better suited), Dot. *The Battle of Life* was also dramatized, by Albert Smith, in December, 1846, Mrs. Keeley playing Clemency Newcome. Tom Taylor's well-known drama, *To Parents and Guardians,* was first produced at the Lyceum, on Monday, the 14th of September, 1846, with Alfred Wigan, as Monsieur Tourbillon ; Keeley, Waddilove ; Mrs. Wigan, Virginie ; Miss Howard, Mary Switch ; and Mrs. Keeley, Bob Nettles. A pantomime, *The Butterfly's Ball,* on Boxing Night, 1846, though written and produced with much elegance, proved, comparatively, a failure, and only ran a few weeks. Shirley Brooks' drama, *The Creole,* was brought out in Easter week, 1847. The only attempt in the strictly legitimate line, was a revival, at Easter, 1845, of Farquhar's comedy, *The Recruiting Officer,* which, as might be supposed, proved quite un-suited to a body of actors trained to such very different work, and was almost immediately withdrawn. The company which Mr. and Mrs. Keeley gathered round them during their three memorable years of management included Messrs. Alfred Wigan, S. Emery, Leigh Murray, Frank Matthews, F. Vining, Meadows, Oxberry, Bellingham, Kinloch, J. W. Collier, Mrs. Alfred Wigan, Misses Woolgar, Fortescue, Fairbrother, Villars, Louisa Howard, Mary Keeley, May, and Isabel Dickenson. They withdrew, owing, as it was said at the time, to some financial disagreement with Mr. Arnold, to the regret of every one, early in the summer of 1847.

The next lessees were Charles Mathews and Madame Vestris, whose reign, extending from the autumn of 1847 to the spring of 1855, however chequered behind the curtain, was certainly one of unexampled brilliancy before it. The theatre reopened under their management on Monday, the 18th of October. It had been superbly redecorated, and one portion of the embellishments, the ornamentation of the box-fronts, on which medallions of cupids, vases, flowers, and birds stood out in strong relief, remains—with a difference of colouring—pretty much as it was, at the present time. The drop-scene, depicting a group of nymphs emerging from behind a mass of crimson drapery, has long since been replaced —but never improved upon. The new company, containing the names of Charles Mathews, Frank Matthews, Harley, Buckstone, John Reeve, R. Roxby, H. Hall, Leigh Murray, Granby, Charles Selby, Meadows, Bellingham, Diddear, C. Horn, Parselle, H. Marshall, Mesdames Stirling, Fitzwilliam, C. Jones, Leigh Murray, Macnamara, Misses Kathleen Fitzwilliam, Louisa Howard, Fairbrother, Marshall, Gilbert, Grove, Laidlaw, and Madame Vestris, was, if anything, too powerful, and therefore, difficult to handle. Its members gradually disbanded,

and moved on elsewhere, Frank Matthews, Roxby, and
Mrs. Macnamara alone continuing with the lessees up to
the close of their management, but, from first to last, there
was always a good working company to be found at the
Lyceum. Mr. Roxby was stage-manager, Mr. Edward
Fitzwilliam, director of the music, and Mr. William
Beverley the principal scenic artist. The opening novelty,
a three-act vaudeville, *The Pride of the Market*, taken
from the French, by Planché, with Vestris as Marton, was
found slight, but—supplemented a little later by *Box and
Cox*, with Buckstone, Harley, and Mrs. Macnamara, and
by Oxenford's little play, *The Tragedy Queen*, with Mrs.
Stirling as Mrs. Bracegirdle—served to carry the house on
till Christmas, which brought with it *The Golden Branch*,
by Planché. This was the first of a series of dramatized fairy tales—fairy extravaganzas their author loved
to style them—which have rendered "the days of Madame Vestris" a unique feature in the annals of the
Lyceum. The others were *The King of the Peacocks*,
The Island of Jewels, *King Charming*, *The Prince of
Happy Land*, *The Good Woman in the Wood*, and *Once
upon a Time there were Two Kings*. The pen of Planché
had long been famous; the pencil of Beverley had
already placed him in the front rank of scene-painters,
but now they were, for the first, and, we believe, the only
time, brought into conjunction, and their efforts guided
and controlled by the master-mind of Vestris, whose
taste and judgment in everything relating to stage-effect
were absolutely faultless. It is not too much to affirm
that such a combination has never been seen since, nor
was it ever seen before. It was the last scene of one of

these extravaganzas, · *The Island of Jewels,* where the simple device was employed of a column of palm-leaves gradually unfolding, and disclosing the regalia of King Emerald bathed in a flood of golden lime-light—which originated the modern pantomime transformation scene— so elaborated, and so utterly vulgarized, since.   Planché, in his memoirs, describes himself as having been alto- gether "painted out" by this scene. We have always held him to be mistaken, and for this reason. His engage- ment with Madame Vestris having come to an end, the last Christmas extravaganza produced under· her manage- ment—in which, by the way, she was too ill to appear— was written by William Brough.   *Prince Prettypet and the Butterfly* was extremely clever, but its wit proved too broad for an audience habituated to the more delicate graces of the elder author, and so, though the mounting was as perfect as ever, it is a fact that the piece did not draw, was withdrawn long before the usual time, and finally the house was closed altogether.

Vestris, then in the autumn—but *such* an autumn—of her days, was still, either as a fairy prince or a *confidante,* or latterly as an old woman, invariably the life and soul of these exquisite *féeries,* acting, to the last, with all her former finish, and singing with nearly all her former charm, whilst the rest of the characters were assigned to the leading members of her company, as constituted at the time.   Amongst these may be specially instanced Harley, as a sort of Arcadian shepherd, *à la Watteau,* in *The Golden Branch ;* Henry Marshall, the never-to- be-forgotten little green dog, Fretillon, of *The King of the Peacocks ;* Frank Matthews and James Bland, the two

acknowledged kings of burlesque ; Mrs. Macnamara, a
veteran actress always at hand for queens or *gouver-
nantes;* Miss Louisa Howard, Miss Kenworthy, and Miss
Agnes Robertson (now Mrs. Dion Boucicault), a beautiful trio of fairy princesses ; Miss Kathleen Fitzwilliam,
and Miss Julia St. George, whose vocal talents were one
of the most important features ; and Miss Rosina Wright,
who, as a guardian spirit or benevolent fairy, invariably
led the dancing in the indispensable ballet scene. Charles
Mathews took no part in these Christmas fairy tales, and
contented himself with merely "playing in " the house,
in one or other of his favourite characters, but he was in
the cast of all the Easter extravaganzas. These—also
written by Planché—were *Theseus and Ariadne, The
Seven Champions of Christendom, Cymon and Iphigenia,*
and *The Queen of the Frogs.* They were produced
with the same completeness, though with less lavish
outlay, had shorter runs, and occupied less of public
attention.

The remaining events of the Vestris and Mathews
management were as follows. Gay's *Beggar's Opera* was
revived in June, 1848, with Madame Vestris, Miss Fitzwilliam, Mrs. C. Jones, the tenor Harrison, Harley, Frank
Matthews, and Meadows. Planché's *BlueBeard*—one of
the old Olympic triumphs—was also reproduced, with
Miss Fitzwilliam, as Fleurette. Buckstone, Mrs. Fitzwilliam, and Mrs. Stirling, quitted the company at the end
of this season. On the reopening, at the beginning of
October, Mrs. Yates had joined, and made her first appearance, to an overwhelming reception, as Tilburina, in
The Critic. Mr. John Reeve, jun., made his *début* soon

afterwards, in a new comic drama, *My Father did so before Me*. On Monday, the 20th of November, Shakspeare's *Merry Wives of Windsor* was revived, with Madame Vestris as Mrs. Ford; Mrs. Yates, Mrs. Page; Miss Fitzwilliam, Anne Page; Mrs. Macnamara, Mrs. Quickly; Granby, Sir John Falstaff; Charles Mathews, Slender; and Meadows, Sir Hugh Evans—a powerful cast. Planché's favourite vaudeville, *A Romantic Idea*, with Charles Mathews, was first produced in March, 1849, and *A Wonderful Woman*, by Charles Dance, in the following May. *The School for Scandal* was revived at the end of this season, with Vestris, Mrs. Yates, Harley, Cooper, F. Matthews, and C. Mathews, and Colman's old musical drama, *Inkle and Yarico*, was given for Harley's benefit, on Monday, the 3rd of July. When the Lyceum opened for the winter season of 1849, Mrs. Yates, Miss Louisa Howard, and Miss Kathleen Fitzwilliam, had left, and were replaced by Mrs. Humby, Miss Kenworthy, and Miss Julia St. George. Miss M. Oliver, and Miss Isabel Dickenson were also added to the company. Charles Dance's comedietta, *Delicate Ground*, was produced in November, with Vestris as Pauline. Mrs. Humby remained for one season, making her mark as Fatima in *Cymon and Iphigenia*, and was succeeded by Mrs. Frank Matthews. Mr. George Vining and Mr. Basil Baker were among the new engagements in the winter of 1850, the principal novelties of which—before Christmas —were, a fairy drama, by John Oxenford, *The Romance of the Rose*, and a melodrama in three acts, by Planché, *A Day of Reckoning*. The latter was a play of much more weight than any new one hitherto given by the manage-

ment, and was admirably got up, but failed in a great
measure, owing to the principal part being intrusted to
Charles Mathews, who was obviously unsuited to it.
Much happier was the result of a version by Slingsby
Lawrence, of De Balzac's *Mercadet*, under the title of *The
Game of Speculation*, in October, 1851.   In this, the Mr.
Affable Hawk of Mathews remained, to the end of a long-
protracted career, one of his best and most popular parts.
The customary extravaganza was superseded at Easter,
1852, by a novelty, in eight acts—taken from the French
by Slingsby Lawrence—with the appropriate title of *A
Chain of Events*.   The varied incidents, the faultless
acting, and the wonderful scenic effects—which included
a practicable ship in a storm—by Beverley, secured for
this unusually long drama a cordial reception and a considerable run.   Miss Laura Keene, a young actress of
much promise, made her first appearance in *A Chain of
Events*.   Planché's *Golden Fleece*—originally produced at
the Haymarket at Easter, 1845—was given here, in October, with Madame Vestris and Charles Mathews in their
old parts, Medea and Chorus, Miss Julia St. George following Miss P. Horton, as Jason.   Mr. Belton, Miss
Eglinton, Miss Wyndham, and Miss Robertson, had now
joined the company.   The Christmas piece, *The Good
Woman in the Wood*, was the most elegant in design, and
the most exquisitely mounted, of all the Vestris series.

At Easter, 1853, Mr. Slingsby Lawrence—in conjunction with Charles Mathews—was responsible for another
long piece, this time described as "A Dramatic Tale in
Nine Chapters," entitled *A Strange History*.   It is difficult to understand why a public who, but a year since,

had so willingly accepted *eight* acts, should now so unanimously reject *nine*. Yet such was the case. The new play was by no means uninteresting, it was full of picturesque situations, and was played, down to the smallest character, most artistically, whilst the scenery was acknowledged to surpass anything hitherto attempted, even by Beverley. We remember an Alpine pass, and hut—whence issued Miss St. George, to sing an Alpine song—with a bridge suddenly carried away by an avalanche, just as the heroine Christina (Vestris) was about to cross it, in search of her children; and an elaborately-constructed woodland glade, with a stream and cascade of real water—as pictures of a beauty entirely unique. Neither avalanche, nor glade, however, nor the numberless "sensations" scattered so freely over the play, sufficed to save it. The action was pronounced too complex, and the personages who took part in it, needlessly numerous. *A Strange History* therefore failed, and its failure was a very heavy blow to the management, which the subsequent success of *The Lawyers*—a version of *Les Avocats*, also by Lawrence — by no means sufficed to redeem.

The popular low comedian from the Adelphi, Mr. Wright, a Mr. Gladstone, and Mr. Frederick Robinson, were amongst the new engagements for the winter. The first of these came out in a little piece with the voluminous title, *The Commencement of a Bad Farce which it is to be hoped will turn out Wright at Last.* It was condemned, because the farce was really a bad one; but independent of this, the actor, whose humour was always of the broadest, proved quite out of his element in the refined atmosphere of the Lyceum. He never took root there, and after a few months very wisely returned to his old quarters. Mr. James Bland was engaged at Christmas, and *A Bachelor of Arts*, a new comedy, in two acts, by a hitherto unknown name, Mr. Pelham Hardwicke, not only supplied Charles Mathews with a part which exactly fitted him, but served to introduce Miss Hughes—now Mrs. Gaston Murray— to the London public, with whom she has ever since remained so great a favourite. A Miss Talbot caused some sensation in March, 1854, by her remarkable personal beauty, in a slight vaudeville, *A Charming Widow*. On Thursday, the 15th of June, was produced an English version of Madame Émile de Girardin's *La Joie fait Peur*, here entitled *Sunshine through the Clouds*, with Vestris, and Frank Matthews, in the parts created by Madame Allan, and Reignier. Vestris embodied with consummate art a *rôle* which, it was said, she literally left a bed of sickness to play. It was destined to be her swansong, and she appeared, for the last time on the stage, in it, for her husband's benefit, on Wednesday, the 26th of July. From that date this gifted and long-admired artist was never seen again in public, and died after a lingering and painful illness, some two years later—on the 8th of August, 1856. The Lyceum opened once more, under Charles Mathews, in November, with a somewhat diminished company, of which the lessee, Mr. and Mrs. Frank Matthews, Mr. J. Bland, Mr. Robert Roxby, Mr. Basil Baker, Mr. C. Swan, Mrs. Macnamara, and the Misses Oliver, Talbot, Fanny Ternan, Harriet Gordon, and Hughes, were the principal members. But the Lyceum had lost its presiding spirit. The Christmas novelty, *Prince Prettypet*, failed to attract after the first few weeks, and at length, utterly disheartened, Mathews suddenly closed the house, abandoning, to use his own words, "the cares of management, at once, and for ever," at the end of March, 1855.

Professor Anderson, "The Wizard of the North," gave his necromantic entertainment, *Magic and Mystery*, at the Lyceum, which had remained shut up all the summer, in September. It was attended with such golden results, that at Christmas he removed to Covent Garden, fired with the ambition of there producing the pantomime of 1855-6. The preliminary announcement of this panto-mime was probably the cleverest theatrical advertisement ever penned. The merit of such things is usually con-sidered to consist in their conciseness.' This one occupied at least a column and a half, and yet every line of it was interesting reading. It made a considerable sensation at the time, and therefore deserves to be put on record here. The author we believe was Professor Anderson's acting-manager [query, or treasurer?]—Mr. E. P. Hingston. The pantomime itself, however, *La Belle Alliance*, though, as a literary effort—it was written by George Augustus Sala —of a high order, failed to come up to the general ex-pectation, and the "Wizard" lost by it all the money previously made in Wellington Street. Finally, Covent Garden was itself burnt down, on the night, or rather morning, of a masquerade, given for his benefit, in March, 1856. The Royal Italian Opera being thus left without a home, Mr. Gye forthwith secured the Lyceum for the

⁷ See the *Times* for Monday, 24th of December, 1855.

season. Wisely eschewing the spectacular operas of Meyerbeer as being unsuited to the smaller arena, the director contented himself with the lighter works of the purely Italian school. *Norma, Lucrezia Borgia, L'Elisir d'Amore, Il Barbiere, Il Conte Ory*, and others, not forgetting *Il Trovatore*, were here listened to with delight, when interpreted by such artists as Grisi, Bosio, Marai, Nantier Didiée, Mario, Gardoni, Tamberlik, Graziani, Tagliafico, and Ronconi. A new tenor, Signor Neri-Beraldi, was also received with much favour. Mademoiselle Cerito danced; and Costa's orchestra was found as perfect in the small, as in the larger house. The off-nights were devoted to the introduction of the Italian actress, Adelaide Ristori, who, though supported by—with the exception of Signor Bellotti-Bon—a very indifferent company, created a profound impression, in the *Medea* of Legouvé, the *Pia di Tolomei* of Marenco, the *Rosmunda* of Alfieri, and in Goldoni's comedy *La Locandiera*. In the autumn a new lessee, for the English drama, was found in Mr. Charles Dillon, an actor whose powers were of a high order, and, at that time, not disfigured by the tendency to rant, in which, during his later years, he was not unfrequently apt to indulge. Mr. Dillon opened with a version, by Mr. Charles Webb, of *Belphegor the Mountebank*, in which he played the showman, to the last, his best and most popular part. The after-piece was a burlesque by William Brough, *Perdita, or the Royal Milkmaid*. The boy, Henri, in the drama, and the Perdita of the burlesque, were intrusted to a very young girl, who has long since risen to the very summit of her profession. The name of this youthful actress was—Marie Wilton.[a] The other performers whom Mr. Dillon had collected were Messrs. Barrett, J. G. Shore, Calhaem, Stuart, and the then little known or appreciated Mr. J. L. Toole, Mrs Weston, Mrs. Buckingham White, Miss H. Gordon, Miss Woolgar, and Mrs. Charles Dillon. The new management seemed to be characterized by much spirit and liberality, in the way of novelties. A new melodrama, *The King's Musketeers*, was tried in October, and another, *The Black Doctor*, in November. Both were adaptations from the French. At the beginning of December, a new and original romantic drama, in five acts, by a new author, Mr. Edmund Falconer, entitled *The Cagot*, had quite an enthusiastic reception. The literary merits of this play were great, and its sentiment fine, but, like all Mr. Falconer's subsequent plays, it was much too verbose. The part of the Cagot-mother, was played by Mrs. Weston, and that of her supposed son, Raoul, by Mr. Charles Dillon, in a very superior style. With Christmas came a burlesque, *Conrad and Medora*, founded upon the popular French ballet, *Le Corsaire*, by William Brough, and chiefly remarkable for the fine scenery of Mr. Fenton. To this burlesque, a short harlequinade was appended, with Tom Matthews as clown. Another new five-act poetical drama, *A Life's Ransom*, by Westland Marston, was very favourably received, in February, 1857, after the run of which, the lessee essayed the parts of Don Cæsar de Bazan, Richelieu, Virginius, and Hamlet, justifying his previous reputation in all. On the

[a] Now Mrs. Bancroft.

termination of the season, early in April, Mr. Dillon
announced its pecuniary success, and the intended re-
sumption of his management, in the coming winter.

Mr. Gye's arrangements for the rebuilding of Covent
Garden being still uncompleted, he again held the opera
at the Lyceum this summer. The leading singers were
the same as last year, with the exception of Mademoiselle
Jenny Ney, who had not been re-engaged, and with the
addition of two young *prime donne*, not hitherto heard
in England. These were Mademoiselle Euphrosyne
Parepa, and Mademoiselle Victoire Balfe, daughter of the
popular composer of that name. Mademoiselle Parepa,
who came out as Elvira in *I Puritani*, was then pronounced
merely promising, but ultimately ripened into a most valuable and complete artist. As Amina in *La Sonnambula*,
Mademoiselle Victoire Balfe, an elegant-looking girl, in
all the bloom and freshness of early youth, was at
once recognized as a thoroughly-prepared singer, who
only needed time for the strengthening and develop-
ment of her powers. Mademoiselle Balfe's professional
career was however terminated within two or three years,
by a brilliant private marriage. Mr. Gye's novelties this
season were *La Traviata* (Verdi), in which Bosio, as the
heroine, showed herself to be as infinitely superior in
singing as she was utterly inferior in acting to the rival
Violetta in the Haymarket, Marietta Piccolomini; and
Fra Diavolo (Auber), given, we believe, for the first time
in Italian, and the success of which—with Bosio, Zer-
lina; Marai, Lady Rocburg; Ronconi, Lord Rocburg;
Gardoni, Fra Diavolo; Tagliafico, Giacomo; and Zelger,

N

Beppo—was perfect. *Fra Diavolo* was probably never better sung, acted, and mounted anywhere than it was at the Lyceum in the season of 1857. Ristori was again engaged, and added to her *répertoire* Camma, in Signor Montanelli's play of that name; Bianca, in an Italian translation of Dr. Milman's fine tragedy, *Fazio;* and Lady Macbeth—in which she was, of course, superb. The popular tenor, Mr. William Harrison, and Miss Louisa Pyne, who had recently returned from America, entered into partnership for a three months' season of English opera in the autumn, with the aid of Madame Caradori, Miss M. A. Prescott, Miss Susan Pyne, Mr. St. Albyn. Mr. George Honey, Mr. Ferdinand Glover, Mr. Weiss, and others, a chorus drawn from the choristers of Covent Garden, and an excellent orchestra conducted by Mr. Alfred Mellon. Their inaugural opera, *The Crown Diamonds* of Auber, on Monday, the 21st of September, testified unmistakably that the word *ensemble* was thoroughly understood, and had been carefully attended to in everything relating to the general execution. The scheme however seemed to languish, until the production of a new opera by Balfe, on Thursday, the 29th of October. This was *The Rose of Castille*, the story of which was identical with that of Adam's *Muletier de Toledo.* Its triumph was immediate and complete. The introductory chorus, "List to the gay castanet," the laughing trio, "I'm not the Queen," and a ballad, "The Convent Cell," so chastely rendered by Miss Louisa Pyne—who was never heard to greater advantage than on this occasion—were among the many bright bits of this very bright and pleasing work; but better than any, to our thinking, was the mule-driver's fresh and tuneful air, "I am a simple muleteer," given in his happiest and most vigorous style by Harrison. *The Rose of Castille* drew immense houses down to the expiration of the Pyne and Harrison term, and secured the financial success of their enterprise. Mr. Dillon resumed his management at Christmas, with a gorgeou oriental spectacle and pantomime on the subject of *Lalla Rookh*, in which Miss Woolgar, Mrs. Buckingham White, and Mr. Toole figured, together with Tom Matthews, who was again engaged as clown. Early in January, 1858, *Lalla Rookh* was preceded in the bills by a brilliant little comedy in three acts, from the pen of Leigh Hunt, with the title of *Lovers' Amazements*, extremely well acted by the lessee, and his wife, Miss Woolgar, and Mr. J. G. Shore. Another new piece, *A Hard Struggle*, by Westland Marston, at the beginning of the ensuing month, though affording full scope for the talents of both Mr. and Mrs. Dillon, was only moderately successful. Miss Helen Faucit was engaged about this time, and appeared as Pauline, in *The Lady of Lyons*, Beatrice, in *Much Ado about Nothing*, and as Lady Macbeth. Mr. Charles Dillon brought his season to a close at the end of March with a revival of Casimir Delavigne's *Louis XI.*, in which he fully sustained his reputation by a very fine impersonation of that most subtle and perfidious of monarchs.

Mr. George Webster opened the Lyceum, for a few weeks, in July, with Mrs. Charles Young—now Mrs. Herman Vezin—in a version of *La Dame aux Camellias*, and later, with the coloured tragedian Mr. Ira Aldridge, in

N 2

Othello. Mr. Aldridge, an actor of merit, had made some sensation, several years before, as Zanga, in *The Revenge*, but had not recently been seen in London. Mr. Webster's management, which was only provisional, was taken up, later on, by Mr. Edmund Falconer—the author of *The Cagot*—for the production of a new comedy, in three acts, *The Extremes, or Men of the Day*, with Mr. Leigh Murray, Mr. Emery, Miss Kate Saxon, and Mrs. Weston, in the leading parts. *The Extremes* was so ' successful, that its writer was enabled to resume the management at Christmas—after a few weeks' interim, during which the theatre was occupied by Jullien— with a new classical extravaganza, by Mr. Robert Brough, *The Siege of Troy*, supported by Mrs. Keeley, Miss Julia St. George, Miss Talbot, Mr. Emery, Mr. James Rogers, and Mr. Charles Young. *The Siege of Troy* was illustrated by some very fine scenery, painted by Mr. William Callcott, and was altogether so magnificently mounted, as almost to recall the days of Vestris. It was found, however, long and dull, and did nothing for the treasury. Madame Celeste was engaged at the beginning of 1857, and came out in a new melodrama, *Marion de l'Orme.* *A Sister's Sacrifice*, founded upon Lamartine's story of *Geneviève*, was the next novelty, for Celeste, Mrs. Keeley, and Emery, to be succeeded, in its turn, by another, *The Last Hope*, written by John Oxenford. All these were well received, but none secured a run. Mr. Falconer evidently counted much upon a new drama of his own, in five acts, *Francesca, a Dream of Venice.* This, which had been for some time an-

nounced, was at length given, on the night of his benefit, Thursday, the 31st of March. *Francesca*—for which
Mr. Callcott had supplied some lovely Venetian scenery
—contained many effective situations, and much good
writing, but was far too long, and so notwithstanding
the admirable acting of Mrs. Charles Young (Francesca),
and Messrs. Falconer and Gaston Murray, it turned
out a failure, and shortly afterwards the house was closed.
After remaining for many months without a tenant, a new
lessee was found in Madame Celeste, who engaged a
company, of which Mr. Walter Lacy, Mr. James Vining,
Mr. James Johnstone, Mr. F. Villiers, Mr. Forrester,
Mr. John Rouse—a new low comedian from Bristol—
Miss Kate Saville, and Miss Julia St. George, were the
principal members. Mr. William West, was stage-
manager, and Mr. William Callcott, scenic artist. Madame Celeste opened the Lyceum, on Monday, the 28th
of November, with an adaptation, by Mr. Charles Selby,
of *Les Enfers de Paris*, which he here placed upon the
boards under the name *Paris and Pleasure*. In this
"*drame fantastique*," as the bills styled it, Celeste sustained no less than seven characters, and was considered
by everybody to have never acted better. At Christmas,
King Thrushbeard, a combination of spectacle and
pantomime, by Mr. Francis Talfourd, with the additional
assistance of Mr. Callcott's scenery, fully sustained the
reputation of this theatre for splendour. Dickens' *Tale
of Two Cities* was skilfully adapted to the stage, by Tom
Taylor, with the manageress as Madame Defarge, in
January, 1860, and ran for some weeks, to good houses.

In March, the old drama of *The Serjeant's Wife*, was revived, with Mrs. Keeley, in her original part of Margot, and Madame Celeste as Lisette. A short time later, a new and very effective little drama, *The Abbé Vaudreuil*, written by Colonel Addison, was produced. Celeste played the Abbé, in her most effective manner. The season terminated soon after Easter. For the reopening, at the beginning of October, Tom Taylor had provided a new comedy, *The Brigand and his Banker*, founded on Edmond About's novel, *Le Roi des Montagnes*. This, although capitally played by Madame Celeste, Mrs. Keeley, Miss M. Ternan, Mr. George Vining, and an American comedian, Mr. Watkins, failed completely, and was superseded in a very few nights by Boucicault's *Irish Heiress*. Miss Lydia Thompson appeared in *Magic Toys*, and a Miss Gougenheim made her *début* as Neighbour Constance, in *The Love Chase*, to the Widow Green of Mrs. Keeley. Bayle Bernard's Adelphi drama, *The Wept of the Wishton Wish* was also revived, and a new play, *Adrienne, or the Secret of a Life*, by Mr. Leslie, produced. A clever actor of Irishmen, Mr. John Drew, came out, in a new version, by Mr. Stirling Coyne, of *Handy-Andy*. Mr. Falconer contributed a most graceful and fanciful Christmas piece, *Chrystabelle, or the Rose without a Thorn*. This was beautifully put upon the stage, and added to its author's literary fame. A new and very good melodrama, *The House on the Bridge of Notre-Dame*, by Rophino Lacy, brought out in February, 1861, was the last novelty of Madame Celeste's management, which terminated in the middle of April, and it was believed that this old favourite of the public had sustained a heavy pecuniary loss.

Her Majesty's Theatre being closed, owing to the sudden retirement of Mr. E. T. Smith, Signor Puzzi and Mr. Mapleson collected the majority of the singers, and gave a short season of Italian Opera at the Lyceum in June and July, with Titiens, Alboni, Giuglini, Signor and Madame Gassier, Vialetti, and a new barytone, Signor Delle Sedie, who proved a real and valuable acquisition. Signor Arditi conducted these performances, the feature of which was the production of Verdi's newest opera, *Un Ballo en Maschera*, for the first time in England, on Saturday, the 22nd of June. The reception accorded to *Un Ballo en Maschera* was enthusiastic, and though now but seldom heard in London, it long remained one of the composer's most popular works. The other operas mounted in this almost improvised, but spirited, little season, were *Il Don Giovanni* (Mozart), *Les Huguenots* (Meyerbeer), *Martha* (Flotow), *Norma* (Bellini), *Lucrezia Borgia* (Donizetti), and *Il Trovatore* (Verdi). In August Mr. Edmund Falconer was again established in his former quarters, with a new drama, *Woman, or Love against the World*, in which Mrs. Charles Young, Mr. Walter Lacy, and Mr. Herman Vezin, sustained the leading parts. This had a run of sixty or seventy nights, and encouraged the manager to bring forward another of his pieces, an Irish drama, in four acts, entitled *Peep O' Day, or Savourneen Deelish.* The great effect of this drama was a scene in the third act, the Foil Dhuiv, or Dark Valley, into which the heroine

Kathleen Kavanagh (Mrs. D. P. Bowers), was enticed by a letter from her husband, George Purcell, for the purpose of being murdered by an agent, in order to facilitate his second marriage with an heiress. The bridge by which she crossed had been cut away by the assassin, but her brother, Henry Kavanagh (Mr. Herman Vezin), and Barney O'Toole (Mr. Falconer) opportunely appeared at the edge of the cliff, and the former, at the moment when all seemed lost, swung himself, by the branch of an overhanging tree, into the chasm, and achieved the rescue of his sister. The effect of this scene—which of its kind was admirably conceived—was immense, and obtained for what was otherwise a rather dull and spun-out melodrama a run of at least twelve months, extending to the middle of November, 1862, when Mr. Falconer's term expired, and he removed to Drury Lane. A burlesque, *Little Red Riding Hood*, by Mr. Leicester Buckingham, had been brought out at Christmas, 1861, containing a very fine panorama, painted by Telbin, of the Lakes of Killarney. On its withdrawal the panorama was still exhibited as an after-piece, during the remainder of the run of *Peep O' Day*.

. The night of Saturday, the 10th of January, 1863, saw the Lyceum again opened, and this time under the management of the popular French actor, Mr. Fechter, who had enlisted under his banner the Misses Carlotta Leclercq, Kate Terry, Henrade, Lavenu, Messrs. George Vining, John Brougham, Henry Widdicombe—the favourite low comedian from the Surrey Theatre—McIntyre, J. G. Shore, F. Charles, Garden, and Raymond.

The new lessee started well, with a redecorated house and a romantic drama, *The Duke's Motto*, adapted from *Le Bossu*, of Paul Féval, by John Brougham. Féchter and that most captivating actress, Miss Kate Terry, were seen to striking advantage in the new play, which was magnificently mounted, and otherwise thoroughly well played by everybody, great or small, concerned in its production. Full of unlooked-for incidents and stirring adventures, *The Duke's Motto* at once hit the taste of the public, and drew an uninterrupted succession of overflowing houses down to the end of the season, in the second week of August. Many improvements had been effected in the machinery and lighting of the stage, in the interval between the first and second season, which commenced on Saturday, the 31st of October. Miss Pauline Leclercq, Messrs. Emery, and George Jordan, were added to the company, which had lost, however, the services of Mr. George Vining. Mr. William West was now stage-manager—a most judicious appointment. The house opened with *Bel Demonio*, a " Love Story, in Four Acts," from the pen of Mr. John Brougham. This turned out to be another version of a French play, already anglicized as *Pope Sixtus V.*, by Dion Boucicault, some years previously at the Olympic. Féchter and his company were all at their best in *Bel Demonio*, the effect of which was enhanced by a very rich and varied *mise-en-scène*, and though scarcely so successful as its predecessor, *The Duke's Motto*, it ran to full houses till Easter, 1864, when, in order to give some rest to the lessee, John Brougham's clever comedy, *Playing with Fire*, with the author, Emery, Shore, Widdicombe, Miss Carlotta Leclercq, and Mrs. Winstanley, was represented for several nights. On Saturday, the 21st of May, *Hamlet* was revived, on a very elaborate scale, with Miss Kate Terry as Ophelia; Miss Henrade the Actress; Miss Elsworthy, Gertrude; Emery, Claudius; John Brougham, Polonius; Jordan, Ghost; G. F. Neville, Laertes; Shore, Horatio; F. Charles, Osric; Widdicombe, First Gravedigger; and Féchter as the Danish Prince. The thoughtful, natural, and picturesque embodiment of Hamlet by this eminently picturesque actor, was already familiar to the London public, but the present revival revealed, in addition, an almost ideal Ophelia in Miss Terry, who now played that character, we believe, for the first time. Another marked feature was the First Gravedigger of Widdicombe. Telbin contributed some very fine scenery for the revival, which presented many novel features in the general arrangement, notably in the Player's Scene, and the Churchyard in the last act. Altogether this production of *Hamlet* was unusually interesting, and would have commanded a much longer run, had not the precarious state of Féchter's health rendered it necessary to close the house, at the end of June.

The winter season began on Saturday, the 22nd of October, with a version, by Mr. Bellew—with suggestions by Charles Dickens and the lessee—of Paul Meurice's *Fanfan, la Tulippe*, under the title of *The King's Butterfly*. The theatre had sustained an irreparable loss by the secession of Miss Kate Terry, but the piece, notwithstanding, was very well rendered by Féchter, Ryder—a new and important acquisition—Widdicombe, F. Charles, McIntyre, Misses Carlotta Leclercq, Henrade, and Lavenu. The scenery was painted by Mr. William Callcott, who illustrated each of the five acts with an elaborately built-up set. The first of these, a Norman village, with a perfectly solid-looking tower, bridge, and a practicable water-wheel, working, in the front, and a glowing autumnal landscape in the background; and in the fourth act, a charming Watteau picture, in the grounds of Versailles, were especially praised. But the long waits between the acts, entailed by the construction of these scenic marvels, were found terribly wearisome on the first night, and possibly contributed in no slight degree to the coldness of the audience. Anyhow, *The King's Butterfly*—another adaptation of which, *Court and Camp*, though less sumptuously mounted, had proved very fairly attractive at the Princess's Theatre in the preceding year—was but frigidly received, and so within a few weeks the manager had to fall back upon his old Princess's success, Ruy Blas. A new version of *Robert Macaire*, entitled *The Roadside Inn*, was produced early in January, 1865, with Féchter as Robert, and Widdicombe, inimitable as Jacques Strop. Mr. Féchter's *corps de ballet* was always very attractive, and a Storm Dance in *The Roadside Inn* was greatly admired, as a *Divertissement des Marguerites* had been previously in the less fortunate *King's Butterfly*. Ryder and Mademoiselle Beatrice appeared as Mr. and Mrs. Haller in the old play of *The Stranger*, in March, and at Easter a new edition of

Paillasse, now called *The Mountebank,* was essayed with much apparent success by Féchter, Ryder, Emery, Widdicombe, Miss Carlotta Leclercq, and Mademoiselle Beatrice. This play, which, as usual, was very well got up, had the further interest of introducing young Féchter as the Showman's Son. *The Mountebank,* however, only ran for two or three weeks, to be replaced by *Don Cæsar de Bazan,* and the ever-welcome *Ruy Blas.* This season, which, though enterprising, had been an acknowledged failure, terminated at the end of May.

Mr. Féchter reopened his house—later than usual—on Monday, the 6th of November, with a new melodrama, in three acts, *The Watch-Cry,* skilfully adapted from the French, by Mr. Palgrave Simpson, in which the lessee was supported by Emery, Widdicombe, C. Horsman, Clifford, Fitzpatrick, and Miss Elsworthy. In the first act, Féchter was to be seen—and heard—as an *improvisatore;* in the second, when supposed to be dumb, he had to go through the entire scene in pantomime, with the exception of once delivering the signal, "Archers of the palace, watch." The actor's wonderful power of facial expression secured the triumph of this act, and ultimately a favourable reception for *The Watch Cry.* Another drama, of a far higher class, also by Mr. Palgrave Simpson, *The Master of Ravenswood,* founded upon Scott's Lammermoor novel, and with which it had been originally intended to open the season, was brought out on Christmas Eve. Féchter was, of course, Edgar Ravenswood, and Miss Leclercq, though perhaps a little mature for the part, made a very graceful, poetical, and lovely

Lucy Ashton. Miss Elsworthy very exactly represented
Lady Ashton; and Mrs. Ternan returned to the stage,
in order to give prominence to the little part of Alice.
Mr. George Jordan was rather too dignified as the
pusillanimous Lord Keeper; Mr. Herman Vezin
excellent as Bucklaw, and Widdicombe equally so as
the adventurous Craigengelt. Mr. Fitzpatrick played
Douglas Ashton, and pretty Miss Lavenu his boy-
brother Henry. Emery rendered this cast most
satisfactorily complete, as Caleb Balderstone. The
Mermaiden's Well and the Kelpie's Flow were amongst
the more conspicuous specimens of Grieve's scenery,
which throughout had been painted in his finest manner.
The final catastrophe had been altered from the one in
novel, and the hapless lovers now went down together in
the quicksand. *The Master of Ravenswood* had, as
indeed it well deserved, a long and triumphant run, extending far on into April, 1866, when *Hamlet* was reproduced, though the other drama was still occasionally
performed. Miss Leclercq, always thoroughly artistic,
was the Ophelia in the new cast of *Hamlet*. Mr.
Addison replaced Mr. Brougham as Polonius, and
Herman Vezin materially strengthened the *ensemble* as
Laertes. Mr. George Jordan now played the Ghost, and
played it well. On Whit-Monday, the 21st of May, a
version of *The Corsican Brothers* was produced, with new
scenery by Grieve. In this version the Opera-Masquerade
preceded the appearance of the Ghost in Corsica, and a
transparency was substituted for the traditional sliding-
trap, in the spectral entrances. Neither innovation was

found to be any improvement, yet the play charmed not-withstanding. Féchter surpassed himself as the twin-brothers, and was most effectively played up to by Jordan as Chateau-Renaud. Herman Vezin made a distinct feature of the small part of Montgiron. The Corsican peasants, Orlando and Colonna, were capitally rendered by Emery and Widdicombe. Mrs. Ternan, Miss Henrade, and Miss Lavenu, respectively repre-sented Madame dei Franchi, Emilie de l'Esparre, and Rosette. Mr. Cormack's arrangement of the dances proved most felicitous, and Grieve's scenery was pro-nounced perfect. *The Corsican Brothers*—preceded latterly by a little piece, *Doctor Davy*, adapted from the French vaudeville, *Le Docteur Robin*, by the now well-known dramatic author, Mr. Francis Albery—ran to the end of the season, which closed on Saturday, the 30th of June, with a performance of *Hamlet*, given for Féchter's benefit, when the Prince and Princess of Wales signified their appreciation of the actor's managerial efforts by being present. Mr. and Mrs. Boucicault occupied the Lyceum in the autumn with a domestic drama, *The Long Strike;* and at Christmas Féchter returned, with his regular company, in a new adaptation of the old Porte St. Martin melodrama, *La Vie d'un Joueur*, under the title of *Rouge et Noir*, prepared by Mr. Henry Leslie, with Féchter as Maurice, and Miss Leclercq, Pauline, in which parts they created a decided effect. As usual Grieve's scenery was much admired. *Rouge et Noir* ran into the ensuing March, when a few representations of *Hamlet* and *Don Cæsar de Bazan* were given; and a little later *The Duke's Motto* was reproduced, with the manager in his great part of Henri de Lagardère, and Miss Henrade as Blanche de Nevers, in which it must be confessed that she formed but a poor substitute for Miss Kate Terry. The theatre closed in May, and re-opened for Féchter's last season, on Monday, the 16th of September, with a revival of Lord Lytton's play, *The Lady of Lyons*, for which Grieve had painted the entirely new scenery. In this the lessee played Claude Melnotte—a part for which he proved admirably suited—Jordan, Beauseant; Addison, Damas; H. Mellon, Deschappelles; Mrs. Henry Marston, Madame Deschappelles; Miss Elsworthy—excellent in a part rather out of her line—the Widow Melnotte; and Miss Carlotta Leclercq, equally excellent, as Pauline. The play had been slightly altered and rearranged from the original, but went extremely well, and was mounted with the same splendour and refined taste which had distinguished every one of the lessee's productions, new or old, at the Lyceum. *The Lady of Lyons* was the concluding effort of Mr. Féchter's management, which terminated, very little, it may be feared, to his financial advantage, though it certainly detracted nothing from his *prestige*, on Saturday, the 16th of November, 1867.

Mr. E. T. Smith, in his time connected with so many places of public amusement, was the next tenant of the Lyceum, which he opened at Christmas, with a pantomime, *Cock Robin*. Mr. Smith's pantomimes were invariably good, and *Cock Robin* formed no exception to the rule. *Narcisse*, a romantic play, fashioned after the manner which Féchter had made so popular, served to introduce a German actor, Herr Bandman, to an English audience, in February, 1868. Herr or *Mr.* Bandman, as he henceforth came to be known, a fine-looking man, and a very showy actor, made a distinctly good impression as Narcisse, and received more or less efficient support, from Messrs. Fernandez, Basil Potter, J. G. Shore, and William Farren, Miss Milly Palmer, and Miss Herbert. The last was, indeed, a most bewitching representative of Madame de Pompadour. Miss Furtado had also a small part in this play, the action of which was supposed to occur in the reign of Louis XV. *Narcisse,* however, though very well received, did not suffice to keep the house open beyond the end of March. A Mr. Fairclough appeared, as Hamlet, at the beginning of the winter season, and in October, *The Rightful Heir,* altered by Lord Lytton from one of his early plays, *The Sea Captain,* was brought out, with Mr. Bandman, Mr. and Mrs. Herman Vezin, and Miss Milly Palmer. *The Rightful Heir* was received, on the first night, with enthusiasm, and afterwards had a considerable run. Mr. Smith produced another pantomime, *Harlequin Humpty Dumpty,* at Christmas, with the since celebrated Vokes' family, and Rowella, as clown. A new and original play, *Life for Life,* by Westland Marston, was given, early in March, 1869, for Miss Neilson, Mr. Herman Vezin, and Mr. Coghlan. This met with much approval from the Press and the public, and ran till the end of April, when Mr. E. T. Smith threw up the management, and the house was once more "to let." An amateur, Mr. Allerton, rented it in the autumn, bringing with him, Mr. Walter Lacy, Mr. Coghlan, Mr. Wybert Reeve, and Miss Kate Saville. The most interesting event of a brief and by no means prosperous season, was the production of *The Syren*, very neatly adapted, by Mr. Palgrave Simpson, from Octave Feuillet's powerful but repulsive play, *Dalilah*. Miss Kate Saville represented the heroine, and Mr. Coghlan made his mark as Count Carnioli. Mr. Allerton played the victim of Dalilah's treachery with much good intention and no little talent, but showed that, as yet, he had nearly all the business of his art to learn.

The Lyceum was next reopened, on Saturday, the 22nd of January, 1872, by the Messrs. Maunsell, with a translation of Hervé's *opéra-bouffe*, *Chilperic*. Although Offenbach's favourite works, such as *Orphée aux Enfers*, *La Belle Helène*, and *La Grande Duchesse de Gérolstein*, had been already given in English at various metropolitan houses, this was, we believe, the first theatrical venture specially devoted to a form of entertainment which has since become so generally popular. On the present occasion, nothing had been left undone to ensure success. The theatre had been thoroughly cleaned and redecorated, a new drop-scene painted, and the opera itself was mounted in the most luxurious and complete manner. Mrs. Keeley also, who had for some time retired from the stage, was pressed into the service, to return for one night and deliver—not without emotion— an appropriate address, contributed by Oxenford, and was greeted with all the honours due to one whose

O

memory was still so affectionately—and so justly—
cherished. Hervé himself played in the new *opéra-bouffe*,
which presented moreover two other new candidates for
public favour—Marius, and Selina Dolaro. The reception given to *Chilperic* was most encouraging, much more
so, indeed, than that accorded to another novelty which
preceded it. This was a satirical comedy in two acts,
Corrupt Practices, by Mr. Frank Marshall. It was surely
a vexatious mischance which caused a work of such real
talent and promise to be put forward as a mere *lever de
rideau* to an *opéra-bouffe*. In spite of the pointed brilliancy
of its dialogue, and some very good acting on the part of
Coghlan, G. F. Neville, G. Vincent, Miss L. Thorne,
and Miss FitzInman, the play fell comparatively flat
with an audience whose interest was centred upon what
they naturally regarded as the important event of the
night. Eventually, however, *Corrupt Practices* righted
itself with the public, and the two pieces then ran well
together up to Easter. At that date, Hervé's *Le Petit
Faust*—in many respects a better work than *Chilperic*—
was brought out, in which a young girl, Miss Jennie Lee,
who subsequently came to the front, showed considerable
aptitude, in the small part of a street arab. The Messrs.
Maunsell relinquished their speculation at the beginning
of July. Mr. Falconer made one more effort at management, in September, with another Hibernian drama,
called *Innisfallen, or the Men in The Gap*. This was
a total failure, and the doors of the Lyceum then
remained closed for the rest of the year, if we except
an unfortunate attempt, on the part of some amateurs,

on Christmas Eve, to perform *A Christmas Carol*, with
Mr. Joseph Stammers as Scrooge. For some cause or
other most of the performers failed to put in an appearance, the result being no performance behind the footlights, and a general uproar in front of them. Mr.
Stammers, who died a few months later, will be best
remembered, as the originator of the once popular
Wednesday Concerts, at Exeter Hall. An Italian company occupied the house early in 1871, and gave several
now almost forgotten operas, such as the *Matrimonio
Segreto* of Cimarosa, and the lovely *Italiana in Algieri*,
and *Cenerentola*, of Rossini, as well as a new one, *Ali
Baba*, by the famous contrebassist, Bottesini, which
notwithstanding the cleverness of much of its music left
no lasting impression. Tito Mattei conducted, and the
operas were rendered in good style, but the only vocalists
above the average, were a Mademoiselle Colombo—now
Madame Mattei—and the buffo, Borella.

After another dreary interregnum, Mr. Bateman, father
of the well-known *tragédienne*, Miss Bateman, became
lessee, and opened with *Fanchette*, a dramatic idyl of
rather slight texture, adapted by Mrs. Bateman from *La
Petite Fadette* of Georges Sand, played by Messrs.
Henry Irving, Addison, G. Belmore, Miss Georgiana
Pauncefort, and a pretty *débutante*, Miss Isabel Bateman,
a younger daughter of the manager. Mr. Irving's performance of Landry, the gloomy lover of Fanchette, was
the leading feature of this piece, which had only a
moderate success. Mr. Charles Warner, a young actor,
who had not as yet found his opportunity—to come

later,[1] elsewhere—also appeared in the farce of *Bamboozling*, and Mr. Bateman brought with him an excellent scenic artist, in Mr. Hawes Craven. *Fanchette* was superseded, at the end of October, by a new version of *Pickwick*, by Mr. James Albery, in which Mr. Irving strengthened the good opinion already formed of him by a life-like portrait of the adventurer, Alfred Jingle. Both these novelties were got up in the most careful and artistic manner, but failed to draw attention, in any marked degree, to the new enterprise. On Saturday, the 25th of November, however, things took another turn, on the production of a new drama, *The Bells*, being an adaptation by Mr. Leopold Lewis of Erckman-Chatrian's *Le Juif Polonais*. The Mathias of Irving immediately created a most profound impression, establishing, in one night, the reputation of the actor and the permanent success of the management. All London went to see *The Bells*, and nothing else was spoken of in the artistic world but the marvellously realistic death-scene of Irving. The play ran for one hundred and fifty consecutive nights, to overflowing houses, and was supplemented, at Easter, by a revival of James Kenney's old farce—written for Covent Garden, in 1803—*Raising the Wind*, with Irving inimitable as Jeremy Diddler. Later on Miss Bateman made her first appearance at the Lyceum, in her great part of Leah, and afterwards played with fine effect, in a new tragedy, in three acts, by Mr. W. G. Wills, on the subject of *Medea in Corinth*, supported by Ryder,

[1] As Coupeau, in the melodrama, *Drink*, produced at the old Princess's Theatre, on Whit-monday, 2nd of June, 1879.

·T. Swinburne, Charles Warner, and Miss Virginia Francis
—another daughter of Mr. Bateman. The second season
of the new management commenced on Saturday, the
28th of September, with a new and very well-written
play, by Mr. Wills, *King Charles I.*, in which Irving
confirmed his position, by a very fine performance of
King Charles, and Miss Isabel Bateman played with much
grace and tenderness, as Queen Henrietta Maria. *King
Charles I.* ran for one hundred and eighty nights, to be
replaced in the spring of 1873, by another new drama,
from the same source, founded on the tale of *Eugene
Aram.* The plot of Mr. Wills differed widely from that
of Bulwer Lytton's novel. Here Eugene (Mr. Irving),
falls in love with Ruth Meadows (Miss Isabel Bateman),
the daughter of the Vicar of Knaresborough, (Mr. W.
H. Stephens), is taxed by Houseman (Mr. Edgar), in
the vicar's parlour, with the murder of Clarke, confesses
his guilt to Ruth, in the churchyard of Knaresborough,
and dies in her arms. *Eugene Aram* was essentially a
play of one part, and that part was exactly fitted to the
idiosyncrasy of Irving, who was seen to the greatest advantage, as the conscience-stricken student. It had at
least a very fair success, and held its own until Miss
Bateman returned to wind up the season with *Medea*.
The next winter brought with it a revival of *Richelieu*, in
which Irving made a powerful effect as the Cardinal, the
house being roused to the greatest enthusiasm by his
magnificent delivery of the imprecation in the fourth act.
He was well supported by Clayton, as Louis XIII., and
by Mr. J. B. Howard, as De Mauprat ; but Miss Isabel

Bateman, though showing much intelligence, was clearly overweighted, as Julie de Montemar.

On Saturday, the 7th of February, 1874, *Philip*, a new romantic play, by Mr. Hamilton Aïdé, was produced. The story of this play bore on the love of two brothers, Philip (Irving), and Juan (Clayton) de Miraflore, for a young French girl, Marie (Miss Isabel Bateman), the *protégée* of their mother. In a fit of jealousy, Philip stabs Juan, as he supposes, and then makes his escape to France. Later, we find Philip married to Marie, whom he suspects of a criminal attachment to a stranger, who has recently appeared on the scene. On the unexpected return of her husband, Marie conceals this stranger in her oratory, and denies that any one has been with her. Phillip orders the door of the oratory to be walled up, whereupon Marie, whilst protesting her innocence, confesses that a man is hidden there. The stranger is dragged forth, tears off his disguise, and reveals himself as the lost Juan. Mutual explanations of course follow, and Juan promises to leave them, and to bury his love in exile for ever, as the curtain falls. Irving and Clayton were alike admirable in their respective *rôles*, and Miss Isabel Bateman played very nicely as Marie. Two slighter parts, the old Countess de Miraflore and a Count de Flamareus, were most artistically filled in by Miss Pauncefort, and Conway. *Philip*, which had the advantage of a very picturesque *mise-en-scène*, had a pronounced success. On Saturday, the 31st of October, *Hamlet* was revived, with Irving, Hamlet ; Swinburne, Claudius ; Chippendale, Polonius ;

T. Mead, Ghost; Conway, Osric; Compton, First Gravedigger; G. Neville, Horatio; Beaumont, Guildenstern; Miss Pauncefort, Gertrude; and Miss Isabel Bateman, Ophelia. In the face of elocutionary defects, at that time apparently insurmountable, Irving yet created an immense effect, in many portions of this tragedy, and especially in the players' scene. Here the agonized manner in which the grief-crazed Prince flung himself upon his father's seat, when the rest of the company had hastily withdrawn, was just one of those "touches" which could not fail to stir the heart of even the coldest and most unimpressionable spectator. Mr. Irving was, upon the whole, extremely well supported. The Claudius of Swinburne, the Polonius of the veteran Chippendale, the Guildenstern of Beaumont, the Ghost of Mead, and the First Gravedigger of Compton, were to be instanced as thoroughly good Shakspearian performances; nor should the Osric, and Laertes, of those younger but rapidly rising actors, Conway and Leathes, be overlooked. Gertrude was, of course, safe in the hands of so judicious and experienced an actress as Miss Pauncefort, but the Ophelia of Miss Isabel Bateman, although invariably painstaking and intelligent, was found to be occasionally unequal. Few, it may here be said, who only witnessed the earlier efforts of Mr. Bateman's third daughter, are probably aware of the excellence to which she subsequently attained. At this initiatory period, whilst the mind and the intention were invariably evident, her extreme youth, and consequent lack of physical strength, rendered her not always able to carry out her aims. A few years later, and at another theatre—New Sadler's Wells—when the requisite time, and experience, had enabled her to realize her conceptions, Miss Isabel Bateman—in parts far heavier than those which she had ever essayed, at the Lyceum—showed that she had developed into a highly accomplished, as well as a most winning and sympathetic actress, and now, unfortunately for the public, whilst still young, and in the maturity of her talents, she has retired, we believe, altogether from the stage. Much had been anticipated, in the getting-up of this revival of *Hamlet*, but in reality very little—comparatively speaking—seemed to have been achieved. The decorations were everywhere appropriate, and occasionally handsome, but they were nothing more. Far less in fact had been effected than was customarily the case under the intelligent direction of the Batemans. The attraction of the new Hamlet, however, may fairly be said to have carried everything else before it, and resulted in the play being retained in the bills, until the 29th of June, 1875, when the house closed for the summer.

Mr. Bateman, the lessee, had died, after a very short illness, on the 22nd of March in this year, but the management was continued by his widow, who reopened, on Saturday, the 25th of September, with a most artistic revival of *Macbeth*, in which Irving appeared as Macbeth; Swinburne, Macduff; Henry Forrester, Banquo; E. H. Brooke, Malcolm; Miss Pauncefort, Hecate; Mead, John Archer, and Mrs. Huntley, the Witches; and Miss Bateman, Lady Macbeth. The Macbeth had many fine points, but on the whole was felt to be a disappointment. The Lady Macbeth of Miss Bateman has at all times been held to be one of her grandest impersonations, and the other parts were all well rendered. As a *spectacle*, *Macbeth* was altogether faultless, and the appearance of the witches, first seen in mid-air during a thunder-storm, through a gap in the clouds, had a most weird and picturesque effect. *Macbeth* continued attractive for many weeks, and in the middle of February, 1876, Mrs. Bateman brought forward *Othello*, on the same liberally-appointed scale; but the Othello of Irving again failed to satisfy expectation. The Iago of Forrester, the Cassio of E. H. Brooke, the Brabantio of Mead, and the Emilia of Miss Bateman, were the best features of this revival, which gave place, in April, to Tennyson's *Queen Mary*, with Miss Bateman as Mary Tudor, and Irving as Philip of Spain. Although an artistic success for Miss Bateman and Irving, who were both seen to the highest advantage, *Queen Mary* proved financially a failure. As a literary effort, the superiority of this play was beyond all question, but it was not adapted for stage-representation, and consequently did not draw. A very creditable reproduction of Mrs. Cowley's old comedy, *The Belle's Stratagem*, with Irving in his favourite character of Doricourt, formed the concluding effort of an energetically conducted season, which terminated on Saturday, June the 24th, when Miss Helen Faucit played Iolanthe, in Theodore Martin's version of *King René's Daughter*, for

Irving's annual benefit. The Lyceum was underlet in the autumn to Mr. Carl Rosa, for English operatic performances. *The Water Carrier* (Cherubini), *Fidelio* (Beethoven), *The Flying Dutchman* (Wagner), *The Lily of Killarney* (Benedict), *Giralda* (Adolphe Adam), *Maritana* (Wallace), and a new opera, *Pauline*, founded on *The Lady of Lyons*, by a young composer, Mr. F. H. Cowen, were the chief features of Mr. Rosa's season. The principal singers were Messrs. Santley, Ludwig, Celli, Aynsley Cook, Packard, Turner, and Charles Lyall, Mademoiselle Torriani, Miss Julia Gaylord, and Miss Josephine Yorke. The dramatic season commenced with *Macbeth*, on Saturday, the 16th of December, and, early in 1877, Mrs. Bateman revived Dean Milman's tragedy of *Fazio*, with her eldest daughter as Bianca, E. H. Brooke, Beaumont, and Mead, in the other parts. *Fazio* had long since been laid aside, but, as a theatrical curiosity, was now found for a few nights interesting, and the Bianca of Miss Bateman deservedly met with many admirers, as did also, and with equal justice, the Fazio of Mr. E. H. Brooke. On Saturday, the 29th of January, 1877, *King Richard III.*, according to the text of Shakspeare—Colley Cibber's version having been wisely discarded by Mrs. Bateman—was produced. Admirable in its comedy touches, but occasionally deficient in tragic power and intensity, the Richard of Irving was, nevertheless, universally acknowledged to be one of his best and most finished efforts. Miss Bateman brought all the force of her faultless elocutionary method to bear upon the part of Margaret, but was generally felt to have rather over-emphasized its tone. On the other hand, Miss Isabel Bateman showed marked progress as Lady Anne, Miss Pauncefort as Elizabeth ; Swinburne, Buckingham ; Walter Bentley, Clarence ; Beaumont, Edward IV. ; E. H. Brooke, Richmond ; Lyons, Hastings ; and Mead as the First Murderer; took great pains with their respective characters. This interesting revival ran till the middle of May, when the old melodrama, *The Courier of Lyons*, took its place, with Irving in the doubled parts of the citizen Lesurques and the highwayman Dubosq, doing the fullest justice to both. For some reason or other, *The Courier of Lyons* was now rechristened *The Lyons Mail*. It ran to the end of a very prosperous season in July. The theatre was opened again at the end of August with a dramatized version of Wilkie Collins' novel, *The Dead Secret*, for Miss Bateman. This was not a success. The regular winter season did not commence till Boxing-night, when *The Lyons Mail* was again performed. The first interesting event of the new year was the presentment of Casimir Delavigne's *Louis XI.*, as arranged by Boucicault. In this, as the French King, Irving deservedly achieved one of his greatest triumphs. A new play by Mr. W. G. Wills and Mr. Percy Fitzgerald, on the subject of *The Flying Dutchman*, and entitled *Vanderdecken*, was produced on Saturday, the 8th of June. Irving's Vanderdecken was a singularly fine study, and Mr. Walter Bentley showed decided ability as Olof, but the piece had only a moderate run. Mr. Irving appeared for the last time during that season, at the end of July. Miss Bateman then returned for a few performances of *Mary Warner*, and at the end of August Mrs. Bateman relinquished her lesseeship to the actor " whose attraction as an artist "—as she very gracefully acknowledged in her valedictory address—had so materially conduced to the financial prosperity of what had certainly been, on the whole, a most spirited and interesting seven years of management.

Having completely, and very handsomely, redecorated the Lyceum, Mr. Irving commenced his management on Monday, the 30th of December, 1878, with *Hamlet*, entirely remounted on a scale of great splendour and elaboration.   There were several important changes in the cast, amongst which we may note that Forrester now played Claudius ; Chippendale, Polonius ; and Swinburne, Horatio.   Mr. Kyrle Bellew was now the Osric, in place of Conway ; and the matchless Compton—who had died during the year before—was succeeded—dare we say replaced ?—by Johnson, an excellent low comedian, as the First Gravedigger.   Lastly, there was a new and most attractive Ophelia, in the person of Miss Ellen Terry.   *Hamlet* ran till the middle of April, 1879, when *The Lady of Lyons* was produced, with Irving as Claude Melnotte; Walter Lacy, Colonel Damas; Forrester, Beauseant; Kyrle Bellew, Glavis; Cooper, Deschappelles ; Johnson, the Landlord ; Tyars, Gasper ; Elwood, Gervais ; Andrews, Desmoulins ; Mrs. Chippendale, Madame Deschappelles ; Miss Pauncefort, the Widow Melnotte ; and Miss Ellen Terry, Pauline Deschappelles.   With much to recommend it, Claude Melnotte could still scarcely be considered as one of Irving's most successful efforts ; and in electing to portray the gentler, rather than the

scornful attributes of Pauline Deschappelles, Miss Ellen
Terry certainly departed from every recognized tradition
of the part. In so doing, however, she may, without
flattery, be said to have originated a tradition of her own,
for the benefit of future representatives, so inexpressible
from first to last, was the charm of her delineation. In
emerging from retirement, to strengthen the cast, as
Damas, Mr. Walter Lacy, by his highly-finished acting
and polished elocution, delighted all old play-goers, and
formed an interesting study for the benefit of younger
ones. *The Lady of Lyons* admirably acted, as a whole,
and very beautifully put upon the stage, had a successful
run of several weeks. Mr. Irving then played a round
of his most popular parts, and brought his first season to
a close on Saturday, the 26th of July. Colman's old
play, *The Iron Chest*, was revived on the reopening of
the house in September. The part of Sir Edward Mortimer, long a favourite with Edmund Kean, as well as,
subsequently, with his son, Charles Kean, and Phelps,
was on this occasion naturally assumed by the manager,
who has seldom played better, or been seen to more
advantage. Barnes, as Fitzharding ; Mead, as Rawbold ;
S. Johnson, as Stephen ; and Miss Pauncefort, as Judith ;
all played remarkably well. Miss Florence Terry made
a very pleasing Lady Helen, and a very young actor, Mr.
N. Forbes, although ineffectively made up for the part,
showed much aptitude as Wilford. Much of the
original music by Storace was retained for the orchestra,
and the production had the further advantage of some
good scenery by Hawes Craven. *The Iron Chest*, how-

ever, was found too gloomy for modern audiences, and made way, in a very few weeks, for a magnificent revival of Shakspeare's *Merchant of Venice.* In this revival Irving's Shylock found many admirers, and a few opponents, though there could be only one opinion as to the amount of care and thought which he had brought to bear upon its study. For ourselves we have always reckoned Shylock among the very finest of his many fine achievements. The Portia of Miss Ellen Terry might be held to want rather more weight, in the Trial-scene, but as a whole completely enchanted her public. Among the other conspicuous performers were Barnes, as Bassanio ; Beaumont, as the Duke of Venice ; Tyars, the Prince of Morocco ; and Johnson, as Launcelot Gobbo; but indeed the entire cast called for nearly everything to praise, and scarcely anything to condemn. The scenery by Hawes Craven, Cuthbert, Walter Hann, and William Telbin was indeed exquisitely beautiful. In May, 1880, *Iolanthe*, a new version, by Mr. W. G. Wills, of *King René's Daughter*, was brought out. This graceful litte idyl afforded a fresh field for the talents of Miss Terry, Mead, and Irving, and also of Mr. Hawes Craven, who provided a wondrously luxuriant garden-scene, for its illustration. To allow, however, of *Iolanthe* being given as an after-piece to *The Merchant of Venice*, the latter was now played in four acts—by the simple expedient of omitting the fifth altogether. The taste of such an arrangement—in a theatre of such real and well-sub-stantiated claims to supremacy in everything relating to

Art—was certainly questionable, and it was paying moreover but a poor compliment to Shakspeare.

Owing to the long-continued attraction of the *The Merchant of Venice*, the reproduction—long expected—of that best of all modern supernatural dramas, *The Corsican Brothers*, was postponed till the opening of the winter season on Saturday, the 18th of September. Mr. Irving retained Boucicault's version, so long and so justly popular at the old Princess's, in place of the one already given, some years previously, by Féchter at the Lyceum. The period of the action, however, was now thrown back to the beginning of the century, with no sort of gain to the general effect, since it entailed a costume the reverse of picturesque or becoming. The elaborate Corsican interior of the first act, also, although a very fine set, was far too bright in colour to form—even with the lights turned down—a sufficiently gloomy framework for the entry of the Ghost; and in the grand scenic display of the second, the interior of the Opera-House, the old theatre in the Rue Lepelletier—always hitherto represented—was now superseded by a *salle*, wonderfully brilliant and realistic, it is true, with its practicable boxes peopled by living occupants, and its fountain of real water in full play, but which in no way resembled any Parisian theatre past or present. The "Clearing of the Forest of Fontainbleau," in the last act, however, was a stage-picture worthy of all praise, and here Irving (Fabien dei Franchi), and Terriss (Chateau-Renaud)— one of the most rising and talented actors of the day—

neither of whom, earlier in the evening, were felt to have entirely come up to expectation, now altogether surpassed themselves, acting and fencing in such a manner as to challenge comparison with the best of their predecessors in Oxford Street, or else where. Miss Fowler, who is invariably prepossessing, made a very tender and pathetic Emilie de L'Esparre, a part rather out of her line. This part is an ungrateful one for leading ladies, its interest being merely transient, and confined entirely to the second act. In bygone days, however, we remember to have seen it made much of by two actresses now vanished from the scene—Miss Murray and Miss Heath. The Masquerade was gorgeous in the extreme, and, as forming one more proof of the manager's boundless liberality in outlay, we may add that the Pierrots who so conspicuously figured in it, were no mere ordinary supernumeraries, but the sons of the celebrated clowns, Rowella, Deulin, Giova-nelli, Waite, Boleno, and Huline. But upon the whole, the splendours of this latest edition of *The Corsican Brothers* appeared to us somewhat overdone. Our old friend, the Ghost, seemed in danger of being finally laid by the force of its own magnificence.

The return of Ellen Terry, at the beginning of 1881, brought with it a new tragedy in two acts, *The Cup*. This was a dramatized form by Tennyson, of a story from Plutarch, which had been already rendered illus-trious by the genius of Ristori in Montanelli's Italian version, *Camma*. Beyond the extremely picturesque act-in~ of Miss Terry, Irving, and Terriss, *The Cup* revealed new scenic glories in a Galatian Landscape, seen under the various aspects of day and night, and a massively built-up Temple of Artemis. On Easter Eve, *The Belle's Stratagem* was given for the first time under the present management, with Irving—in his happiest vein—as Doricourt; and Miss Ellen Terry—a most charming Letitia Hardy. Mrs. Cowley's comedy served also to introduce that old and experienced actor, Mr. Howe, to the Lyceum boards as Hardy. In May the famous American tragedian, Booth, was engaged to alternate with Irving the parts of Iago and the Moor, in Shakspeare's *Othello.* Matured by years of study, the Othello of Irving showed a very great advance upon his earlier attempts in that part, but it was in the far more difficult and subtle character of Iago, that he was seen to the greatest advantage. The triumph of the English actor, no less than that of his transatlantic brother-artist, was here universally admitted. In other respects Booth had the advantage of much better professional support than had been the case in his previous appearances [7] elsewhere. The Cassio of Terriss, the Brabantio of Mead, and the Duke of Beaumont, were all impersonations far above the average. Needless to add that Miss Terry was Desdemona. The mounting of *Othello*, though without profusion, was rich and appropriate, and the entire scheme redounded greatly to the artistic feeling and spirit of the manager. In the autumn the house was sublet to an Italian Opera company, under the musical guidance of

[7] At the new Princess's Theatre, during the winter months of 1880-81.

P

Signor Li Calsi. The only singers of any eminence were Marimon, Rose Hersée, the barytone Padilla, and the tenor Frapolli. The experiment, however, did not answer, and was soon abandoned.

When the Lyceum reopened at Christmas, Albery's excellent comedy, *Two Roses*, first produced at the Vaudeville in 1870, was added to the theatrical repertory. Irving resumed his original character of Digby Grant, with well-merited success, and Mr. David James was expressly retained for that of "our Mr. Jenkins." Howe played Mr. Furnival; Terriss and a new actor, Mr. George Alexander, were respectively Jack Wyatt and Caleb Deecie. Miss Pauncefort was "our Mrs. Jenkins," and the Misses Helen Matthews and Winifred Emery made two very pleasing representatives of the heroines. *Two Roses* pleased greatly, but was withdrawn to make way on Wednesday, the 8th of March, 1882, for a revival, on a very grand scale, of Shakspeare's *Romeo and Juliet*, with the subjoined cast :—

Escalus, Prince of Verona	. .	Mr. Tyars.
Paris {	a young Nobleman, kinsman to the Prince }	Mr. G. Alexander.
Montagu { Capulet {	Heads of two Houses, at variance with each other }	Mr. Harbury. Mr. Howe.
Romeo, son to Montague	. .	Mr. Irving.
Mercutio {	Kinsman to the Prince, and friend to Romeo }	Mr. Terriss.
Benvolio {	Nephew to Montague, and friend to Romeo }	Mr. Child.
Tybalt, Nephew to Lady Capulet	.	Mr. Glenny.

Friar Laurence, a Franciscan .	. Mr. Fernandez.
Friar John, of the same Order	. Mr. Black.
Balthazar, Servant to Romeo .	. Mr. Hudson.
Sampson } Servants to Capulet	{ Mr. F. Archer.
Gregory }	{ Mr. Carter.
Abram, Servant to Montague .	. Mr. Lowther.
An Apothecary . . .	. Mr. T. Mead.
Chorus	. Mr. Howard Russell.
Peter	. Mr. Andrews.
Citizen	. Mr. Harwood.
Lady Montague, Wife to Montague	Miss H. Matthews.
Lady Capulet, Wife to Capulet	. Miss L. Payne.
Juliet, Daughter to Capulet .	. Miss Ellen Terry.
Nurse to Juliet . . .	. Mrs. Stirling.

The Romeo was in one sense, perhaps, a disappointment to those who had gone to the theatre with the conviction that Irving could do no other than fail in a part so completely out of his ordinary line. The result, however, went to prove that if no new triumph had been absolutely gained, there was, on the other hand, no such word as failure to record. If the popular tragedian, like every one of his most gifted predecessors, could scarcely be said to have altogether succeeded in his gallant endeavour to realize an almost impossible ideal, there was nevertheless much—frequently *very* much—both to praise, and to admire, throughout his entire assumption, and more particularly in the latter portions of it, whilst certain mannerisms of style—shortcomings shared in common with every other great actor—for which he had been often previously censured, were only conspicuous by their all but total absence now. With the remembrance, still fresh, of the lamented Miss Neilson, a spirit of hyper-criticism, and even of detraction, might doubtless be apparent in many who followed the progress of the new Juliet. Yet when the curtain fell upon the last act, it was agreed, without one dissentient voice, that although some scenes might very possibly have been less happily treated than others, the same ineffable gift of charm, so pre-eminently distinguishing everything which Miss Ellen Terry has ever touched, had once more been most abundantly manifested, from first to last, by that truly fascinating actress, here. At so recent a date it appears unnecessary to dwell upon the individual merits of the remainder of the cast, since this was exhaustively done at the time by every leading journal of the day. It will be sufficient to say that all did their best with the work, great or small, assigned to them, and that the word " best " should be understood to imply that the highest available standard of excellence had been secured for the rendering of every character. The primary idea, moreover, seemed to be the avoidance of anything which might cause any one part to stand out with undue prominence at the expense of the others, and on the contrary, to secure, as far as possible, the perfect blending of the company in one harmonious whole. We cannot, however, refrain from devoting a few words of special notice to the one who at present may very properly be regarded as the Mother of the Stage—we allude to Mrs. Stirling. No such embodiment of the Nurse of Juliet has, in truth, been witnessed for many years past

in London, nor could it, we imagine, have well been surpassed by any actress at any period in the history of the
British drama. It was, indeed, such a Nurse as Mrs.
Marston, Mrs. Glover—nay even Mrs. Davenport's self—
would have loved to look upon. It afforded to younger
playgoers the opportunity of witnessing a very just specimen of the old, as distinguished from the new, school of
acting. And it added one more, and that a distinctly
marked source of attraction to the many which served
to make up the well-deserved triumph of a truly unique
production. For the rest, this revival of *Romeo and Juliet*
lingers in our memory like the recollection of some beautiful dream. It was not that the pictures—exquisite as
they were—of Hawes Craven, Cuthbert, Walter Hann,
and Telbin, had not been already equalled by themselves,
or other artists, here or elsewhere, but that the various
scenes, by the adroit manner in which the lights were
lowered during their removal, seemed actually to melt
into each other, whereby their dreamy nature was sen-
sibly heightened and consistently maintained throughout.
The dresses, too, were not only of the richest materials,
but so admirable was the mingling and contrast of
colour, that the effect of each stage-picture proved
absolutely faultless. Rare skill also was observable in
the drilling of the supernumeraries, notably in the
Market-Place, with its ever-shifting stream of nobles and
citizens; in the glittering ball-room, with its crowds of
courtiers, and its lovely torch-dance, with the dancers in
white and gold; and in the grouping of the populace on
the staircase of the Capulets' Tomb. The manager had

evidently profited by the visit of the Meiningen Company to Drury Lane during the preceding summer—and had even improved upon the example then set. It is scarcely too much to say that the entire representation of *Romeo and Juliet* at the Lyceum was, in the abstract, simply the perfection of High Art.

Romeo and Juliet ran, without intermission, to the close of the season, at the end of July, 1882. It was reproduced when the house reopened for the winter, on Saturday, the 2nd of September, and was ultimately withdrawn, to make room for another of Shakspeare's plays, the comedy of *Much Ado about Nothing*, on Wednesday, the 11th of October, in the same year. In this revival, Irving as Benedick, and Miss Ellen Terry as Beatrice, were at once admitted to be altogether at their best, winning unstinted approval at the hands of the critics, and almost measureless applause from a most enthusiastic and densely-crowded house. With the omission of Mrs. Stirling, for whom indeed there was no part, and the addition of Mr. Forbes Robertson, engaged for Claudio, the other performers in *Much Ado about Nothing* were nearly identical with those already seen in *Romeo and Juliet*, and played with the same care and finish, as before. In all that regarded the accessories of the stage, the same lavish outlay might be discerned, tempered by the same judgment, and the same faultless taste. Nor was there any difference perceptible in the pictorial effects, save that the sunny landscapes and sapphire seas of the Sicilian coast naturally authorized a greater warmth of colour, than would have been appropriate, in the more sombre surroundings of cypress-clad Verona. The one revival, in short, impressed the audience equally with the other—than which no higher praise could possibly be accorded.

Within a few weeks from the withdrawal of *Much Ado about Nothing*, the present intellectual direction of the Lyceum, falls, for a time, at any rate, into abeyance. Mr. Irving goes with Miss Terry, and his company, to the United States, in the autumn, on a starring tour, of some duration, leaving his theatre, meanwhile, in the hands of the American speculator, Mr. Abbey, who is scarcely likely, we fancy, during a temporary occupation, to conduct it on the same artistic principles. Whether our great Actor-Manager, at a later period—it is said next year—will find himself able to take up the thread of popular interest at the point where he left it, remains to be seen, but to judge from past examples, the outlook is not, we fear, altogether unfraught with danger. We have no desire, however, to foreshadow evil for one to whom the English public is so greatly indebted. We would rather wish him, and his artists—for artists, one and all, in truth they are—their full measure of success in the New Country, together with a speedy and safe return to the house—so rich in its reminiscences—which in the interests of playgoers, it is to be hoped, may long remain their resting-place—the third of THREE LYCEUMS.

THE END.

www.ingramcontent.com/pod-product-compliance
Lightning Source LLC
Chambersburg PA
CBHW030125030726

47498CB00007B/2560